Iconic Restaurants

OF

KANSAS CITY

Iconic Restaurants

OF

KANSAS CITY

ANDREA BROOMFIELD

AMERICAN PALATE

Published by American Palate
A Division of The History Press
Charleston, SC
www.historypress.com

First published 2022

Manufactured in the United States

ISBN 9781467145862

Library of Congress Control Number: 2021952413

Contents

Preface

Kansas Citians hold cherished restaurants close to their hearts, treating them as extensions of themselves and the place they call home. They remain loyal to their favorites, often for as many generations as the restaurants remain in operation. For those that finally do close their doors, they are mourned like family members and friends. This book aims to recall those lost restaurants—for reasons of our collective nostalgia, yes, but also to show how Kansas City's culinary identity and heritage came to be. This book also serves to help us build off that heritage in the new restaurants that open, thus further strengthening our city's distinctive culinary identity.

There are two Kansas Cities: the larger Kansas City, Missouri, and the smaller Kansas City, Kansas. While the two have separate histories, they share many commonalities, given their codependency when it came to the provisions and crossroads hospitality industries that built them both. Often, the state line hardly mattered, and both cities were home to the cherished lost restaurants that are featured in this book.

The most difficult decision I encountered when writing *Iconic Restaurants of Kansas City* was determining which restaurants to include. A strict word count meant that several venerable restaurants had to be excluded. This was exacerbated by the fact that some of the area's restaurants closed during the COVID-19 pandemic, when this book was in production. For ongoing histories of other Kansas City iconic eateries and their histories, please follow my blog at https://www.andreabroomfield.com, on Facebook at www.facebook.com/andrealynnbroomfield and on Instagram at www.instagram.com/kc_lost_and_iconic_restaurants.

The restaurants included in this book explicitly laid our culinary foundation, represent important turning points in our culinary history, were usually family-owned or local and typically survived for more than one generation. There are, of course, exceptions—restaurants that might have been shorter-lived but that pushed our culinary boundaries and challenged us to consider new ways of thinking about food and eating food at restaurants. In every case, the restaurants featured in this book served more than just great food: they offered patrons the intangibles that made dining out special, including celebrations for rites of passage, recreation and community.

Acknowledgements

Many people helped me write this book and are acknowledged in the endnotes. A special thank you to Michael Wells and the librarians at Kansas City Public Library's Missouri Valley Special Collections, who assisted me through all steps of the process, including the many scans of archives that made the research possible, despite COVID-19 lockdowns. Henry Voigt, the curator of one of the nation's most important private restaurant menu collections, likewise offered me much assistance. Chad Rhoad, Ashley Hill and the editors at The History Press ensured that this book came to fruition. The journalists, particularly restaurant critic Charles Ferruzza, wrote the stories that were critical to me as I stitched together the history of many lost restaurants. My father and stepmother, Charles and Marsha Broomfield; my sister, Leah Hyatt; my husband; and my children, Clara and Gavin; likewise shared vital recollections that were essential to the creative process. Thanks as well to Danny Alexander, Emily Behrmann, Ken Behrmann, David Davis, Diane Davis, Julie Haas, Bobby Hackworth, Nancy Ingram, Ted Meadows, Jasper Mirable, Cathleen O'Neil, Heather Paxton, Aaron Prater, Erica Reynolds, Larry Reynolds, Michelle Riley, Arron Small, Allison Smith, Gretchen Thum and Jesse John Vega Jr. for your inspiration, emotional support and cheerleading. This book is in memory of Valters Vittands, who never questioned that I would someday write books.

1

Hostelries and Taverns of Old Westport, Westport Landing and Quindaro

WESTPORT

The area's oldest eateries did not exist in Kansas City, Missouri. That name for the city did not come about until 1889, and when Daniel Yoacham ran his tavern and hostelry in Westport in the 1830s, not even the name "Westport" was official. After John Calvin McCoy came to the vicinity of Kawsmouth (where the Kansas, or Kaw, River empties into the Missouri River) to build his provision post, he called the area West Port—literally a portal to the West. More specifically for his objectives, McCoy situated his business just one mile from Indian Territory. The year was 1833, and McCoy saw economic potential in catering to displaced Native Americans. He subsequently bought up surrounding land and platted it, and his village began to grow.[1]

As McCoy experienced the tediousness of trekking roughly twenty miles to Independence, Missouri, to buy store supplies, he also realized that Santa Fe Trail traders likewise encountered the same obstacles. Using his surveyor skills, McCoy scouted out a sturdy rock landing on the Missouri River near the foot of today's Grand Boulevard. It was roughly two miles west of the already established Chouteau Landing and roughly four miles from McCoy's store. With the use of his enslaved men and hired men, McCoy improved an already existing French trace, carving a road through a break in the bluffs to his store. Meanwhile, he negotiated with a St. Louis steamboat captain to drop off his provisions at what quickly became known as Westport

Landing.[2] McCoy's arrangement showed entrepreneurs the potential of the surrounding bottoms for building shops, hotels and eateries, all of which would begin catering to passengers who were stepping off steamboats to outfit themselves and rest before going west. Westport, meanwhile, overtook Independence to become the eastern terminus of the Santa Fe Trail.

Along with the Chouteau family, McCoy and other early entrepreneurs gave Kawsmouth a reason for existing: provisioning and hospitality. As such, the history of Kansas City restaurants began long before Kansas City existed, and from the earliest days, all manner of hostelries, hotels, taverns and eateries catered to visitors and locals alike.

The area's first hostelry of repute was Yoacham's Tavern, located near today's Mill Street and Westport Road, and it was in operation from roughly 1838, when Daniel Yoacham received a deed for the land, through the 1850s. Daniel Yoacham (also Yocum or Yoacum) and his family came to the area from Tennessee around the time that the Osage tribe ceded its rights to land that, by 1826, had been platted as Jackson County, Missouri. Shortly thereafter, pioneers like the Yoacham family poured into Missouri from the southern states in search of productive land. Yoacham ran his tavern with the help of his wife, Rosannah Campbell May, servants and/or enslaved people and the family's children. Its location near Mill Creek ensured clean water for the tavern's and travelers' needs.[3]

The most humorous account of meals likely served up by Yoacham was offered by Edward R. Schauffler in a 1945 article for WHB's *Swing* magazine, roughly a century after the tavern closed but not before it had faded entirely from people's memories. At Yoacham's, a man "could buy overdone beef and raw whiskey, biscuits, corn bread, sow belly, coffee, beans. Daniel must have been a two-fisted man to have survived his customers, and they needed to be copper-lined to endure his whiskey," Schauffler humorously speculated.[4]

Yoacham's reputation indeed rested with whiskey and its "rakehell" reputation (in Schauffler's parlance). Due to the Santa Fe Trail, significant volumes of money came through the area. Yoacham served as justice of the peace, but that did not stop a group of bandits from using his tavern in April 1843 to plan the murder of wealthy trader Don Antonio José de Chavez. Weeks after the bandits paid their bill (or not) and left Yoacham's, Chavez was found murdered on the Little Arkansas River's banks (north of present-day Wichita). Missing from his body and wagon was upward of $34,000 worth of Mexican silver. Because it was well known that Chavez was on his way to Missouri, a posse of Jackson County citizens—who may have

Harris House at the time of the Civil War. Westport, 1812–1912 *(Kansas City, MO: Franklin Hudson Publishing Company, 1912).*

likewise rendezvoused at Yoacham's—intercepted some of the bandits near Council Grove, Kansas. Ten were caught and hanged or sent to prison, and a portion of the money was recovered.[5]

At some point, Allen B.H. McGee recognized that Yoacham's was perpetually full of customers, and he saw potential in the tavern and hostelry business. In 1846, McGee opened his own tavern at the (now) northeast corner of Westport Road and Pennsylvania Avenue. McGee's operation caught fire the same year he built it, and perhaps because of discouragement or boredom, McGee sold his tavern license to Kentucky native John "Jack" Harris, who, along with his family and enslaved people, built a large two-story log building and named it Harris House.[6] Jack Harris, according to early Kansas City historian Carrie Westlake Whitney, catered to two kinds of people: whiskey drinkers and carousers out in the stable yard and genteel folk who repaired to the Harris House's dining room for meals and conversation.[7]

When fire also destroyed the Harris House in 1851, its reputation for fine food had grown so wide that Westport citizens pitched in to help Jack rebuild, this time three stories in brick. And in 1853, when the Harris House reopened, its reputation was further enhanced by the great cooking of the enslaved Minerva and Mark.[8] While Minerva made corn bread, beaten biscuits, pies and cakes, Mark presided over the meat, roasting and carving venison, wild turkey, cured hams and roast pig, "with a flourish and distinction that made him famous," wrote Whitney.[9] Nellie McCoy Harris offered a firsthand account: "Think of a village tavern with a large patronage, serving hot waffles, buckwheat cakes, chicken pie, fried chicken, turkeys, broiled vension [sic], prairie chicken, buffalo steak, and such other toothesome [sic] viands! These were supplied at all times at the Harris Inn." It became Westport's leading hotel, "famed far and wide for its generous hospitality and southern cooking; every traveler of note who was not privately entertained stayed at the Harris House Hotel," wrote Whitney. Its guests included celebrity author Washington Irving.

The Harris House's cooking style resonated with Kansas Citians long after Jack Harris resigned as its innkeeper, with him and his family wisely leaving when the hotel was commandeered by the Union army during the Civil War. Although Jack leased the Harris House after the Civil War and kept its name and operations going, the dining days of old Westport were gone—but newspaper articles and memoirs fondly recalled the food. By the early 1910s, the property was owned by James and Ella Carr, who met resistance from the Westport Historical Society and other organizations when they planned to raze the building. Locals, instead, wanted to remodel and revive the "antebellum style of cookery" that had made it famous. The deal never went through.[10] The building was sold to developer Victor Laederich in 1922. Even with its decrepit state, emotions ran high when he had the building torn down. As late as 2001, David Baumgartner in *Kansas City Magazine* reminisced about the Harris House—how, during its day, it set the standard for Kansas City's love of fried chicken dinners and fresh-caught catfish.[11]

Westport Landing, the Levee and Eating in the City of Kansas

Yoacham's Tavern and Harris House went down in history as much for the dangers they faced residing on the "Edge of Civilization" (official federal language) as they did for their food. And the same situations confronted those along the levee as well. McCoy's steamboat was soon joined by many more vessels as pioneers and forty-niners heading to California disembarked to outfit themselves on the levee for their journeys west. All of them needed food, lodging and provisions for their journeys.

Critical to sustaining the levee's growth was investment in its infrastructure. John Calvin McCoy joined his father-in-law, William Chick, and a group of investors known as the "Historic 14" to form the Town of Kansas Company. They then began building docks and platting their town, relying extensively on what had been Gabriel Prudhomme's farm and property, acres that extended to present-day Broadway Boulevard, Troost Avenue and Independence Avenue. By 1853, a formal charter gave the town a new name: the City of Kansas.[12]

Among the town's first lodging and food options was Troost House. Built by Dr. Benoist Troost, with help from William Gillis (sometimes Gilliss), the operation was located between Wyandotte and Delaware Streets and was considered acceptable enough for women to reside there. In its first iteration, Troost House offered sixty-four apartments, but between 1850 and the 1890s, when it was converted into a pickle factory, the hotel expanded, frequently changed owners and also frequently changed its name.

The food was rough-and-ready, and as such, few comments regarding it remain. However, those that do are important, because they came from Pennsylvania native and abolitionist Sarah Coates, the wife of Kersey Coates, a Union supporter who was to become Kansas City's first prominent

Gillis House (1867) full frontal and side view. *Courtesy of Missouri Valley Special Collections, Kansas City Public Library (Kansas City, MO).*

restaurateur and hotelier. While Sarah resided at Troost House in 1856, Kersey went about looking for land on which to build a home, an opera house and a hotel.

Around that time, the hotel was bought or leased by the New England Emigrant Society and was often referred to as the American House or Hotel. It was packed with pioneers who were heading west, East Coast Free Soilers on their way across the river to Kansas and border ruffians who supported states' rights. The only thing that united them was their need to eat. The American House, Sarah Coates wrote, is "conspicuous on the levee…a large four-story-and-a-half brick building surmounted by a steeple containing a large bell, whereby the signal is given for rising in the morning and for attendance at meals.…A long table was set, capable of holding fifty or sixty persons."[13] At least during May, guests could enjoy the bouquets of "pineys," or peonies, that graced the long table and freshened the air.[14]

A *Kansas City Star* article noted that during these formative years, the hotel might well have been "hospitable [and] ably conducted," but "thrift was its watchword. Many who later became citizens of influence and substance got their discouraging impressions of the clay-bank city from the…windows."[15] Mealtimes were a chaotic "boardinghouse reach," with "thrift" resulting in an abundance of greasy pork steaks, wild greens, corn pone, catfish from the "Muddy Mo" (another name for the Missouri River), and various grunts and cobblers made of wild fruit.

In 1864, when William Gillis bought the American House, it became the Gillis House. With the Civil War raging, Gillis likely had as little control over his property as Jack Harris had over his; the Union army commandeered the Gillis basement to hold Confederate prisoners who were taken during the Battle of Westport. By 1870, the property had fallen on still harder times. The leveling of the bluffs that separated the levee from what was becoming downtown Kansas City, Missouri, had largely been accomplished, and trains replaced steamboat traffic and its passengers essential to the Gillis House profits. In 1888, historian Theodore S. Case described Gillis House this way: "The business part of the town has long since left this locality, and the old hotel stands lonely and desolate at the foot of the bluffs, a habitation for tramps and rats, both human and animal."[16] By the 1890s, the Gillis House had become a pickle factory, and in 1909, the building was demolished. Nonetheless, memories of it live on due to its significant role in housing and feeding thousands of pioneers, traders, forty-niners and Free Soilers. Food-wise (and drink-wise), Gillis House defined the Town and the City of Kansas before "Kansas City" was officially adopted as the city's name in 1889.

SATISFYING HUNGER ON THE KANSAS SIDE OF THE STATE LINE

Quindaro House (1857–circa 1861)

When the Kansas-Nebraska Act opened Kansas to European settlement in 1854, violence was inevitable, as both supporters of slavery and Free Soilers poured in, determined to shape the territory in their respective images. Initially, Kansas-side landings on the Missouri River were difficult for anyone other than proslavery supporters to disembark. Quindaro was the exception, established on January 1, 1857, as "a friendly port for antislavery partisans to enter and leave Kansas," wrote Alan W. Farley.[17] To discourage passengers from traveling there, steamboat companies supported by the proslavery faction charged exorbitant fees for a stop at Quindaro, as opposed to slavery-friendly ports, such as Leavenworth. Nonetheless, as the Free Soilers wrested control of Kansas away from the proslavery forces, Quindaro's fortunes rose.

During the Border Wars preceding the Civil War, the options for eating away from one's home were fewer on the Kansas side, but one place stands out: Quindaro House, likely the first permanent structure built in what quickly became a boomtown. Quindaro was centered on a rock ledge boat landing on the Missouri River, scouted out by Ohio native Abelard Guthrie. Guthrie's wife, Quindaro, was part of the Wyandot tribe, on whose land the town was located. Abelard named the town after her.

Run by Philip T. Colby and Charles S. Parker (the town's first justice of the peace), Quindaro House was a commanding structure—four stories tall with forty-five rooms—complete with a dining room, storerooms, a mercantile store and a basement for hosting town hall meetings. Almost immediately, settlers voted to make their town dry, setting up a stark contrast to the carousing drunkenness that often characterized the City of Kansas, Missouri.[18] Town prohibitionists destroyed whiskey barrels and stills, including one located in a hollow west of Quindaro House. In that instance, thirty women petitioned the Quindaro City Council, and "the offending barrel was hauled from beneath its owner's bed and spilled out into the street," as Farley related in *Annals of Quindaro: A Kansas Ghost Town.*[19]

Located on Kansas Avenue, Quindaro House was a hive of activity and the gathering place for abolitionists who relied on it for hosting literary societies, balls and banquets. Just after Quindaro House opened, thirty-six steamboats docked there each week to unload scores of Free Soilers who were planning to stay in Quindaro before claiming homesteads in

Lawrence, Kansas, or Topeka. A correspondent from Lawrence, T.D.T., wrote glowingly in 1857: "I passed the night at my usual quarters, the Quindaro House, kept by Messrs. Parker & Colby, and whose merits I have heretofore had occasion to commend. For quietness, neatness, good table, &c., I do not know of a better house in Kansas." Another correspondent ended his column "On the Wing" by urging travelers "who come this way to pay the Quindaro House a visit." There, he said, they would find the hosts "obliging and courteous, and their table is decidedly the best supplied at which we have been seated in Kansas."[20]

A Quindaro newspaper reporter commemorated Thanksgiving in 1857 by considering how many New England families sat down to dinner in Massachusetts, Connecticut and Vermont with seats around their tables empty due to loved ones seeking homes in "Kanzas"; at least they were able to spend the holiday at Quindaro House, where the "worthy hosts" spread "their tables with an ample feast."[21]

By 1858, Quindaro House and the town itself fell on hard times, as it was no longer the sole abolitionist refueling station on the Kansas side of the Kansas and Missouri Rivers. Boats then brought Free Soilers to all Kansas River and Missouri ports, and Abelard's Quindaro Company, which had financed many of the buildings, was bankrupt. While Quindaro would go on to play an essential role in the story of emancipation (the building of Freedman's University was approved by the Kansas legislature in March 1870), the days of dining and edifying lectures at Quindaro House were all but forgotten.

2
Arrival by Rail and Flight

KANSAS CITY'S HOTEL, RAILWAY AND AIRPORT EATERIES

The Hannibal & St. Joseph Railroad Bridge, the first to cross the Missouri River, opened with fanfare on July 3, 1869. That bridge cemented Kansas City's identity as a major crossroads. A year prior to the bridge's opening, the Broadway House (soon to be the Coates House) opened on the southeast corner of Tenth Street, giving Kansas City its first luxury hotel and restaurant.

Dining out became associated with stand-alone restaurants during the twentieth century, but early on, Kansas City's numerous hotels, along with its train station, often had better finances to treat guests to fine cuisine. While travelers could take advantage of so many dining options, so, too, could locals, making Kansas City residents among the nation's first to take Sunday dinner outside of their homes.[22] They expected excellent food at whatever price point—expectations that compelled caterers to reach high standards in order to compete.

When the trains ceased regular passenger service and Union Station's Fred Harvey Restaurant was no longer open, the Charles B. Wheeler Downtown Airport (then the Municipal Downtown Airport) picked up the slack. Meanwhile, downtown hotel restaurants thrived. Soon after their planes landed, visitors checked into the Muehlebach Hotel and stepped into the Terrace Grill for dinner and dancing, or they dropped off their luggage at Savoy Hotel and took dinner in the fabulous grill there. Meanwhile, hotel restaurants stretched to Eighteenth and Vine Streets, where pedestrians crowded sidewalks, listening to the music that spilled into the streets. Many factors contributed to hotel dining's eventual decline, but this chapter relives its glory days, moving chronologically through eateries associated with the city's tourism industry.

EARLY LUXURY DINING:
COATES HOUSE, HOTEL BALTIMORE AND THE SAVOY

Coates House Hotel

Although its construction began in 1857, the Coates House was not completed until 1868–69 due to the Civil War. While catering to the remaining Santa Fe Trail traffic, Coates House also took advantage of railway traffic. Visitors relied on the Kansas City Cable Railway's Ninth Street incline to take them from the Union Depot in the West Bottoms almost to the doorstep of the Coates House.[23] Coates Opera House, next to the hotel, added additional business.

In June 1873, Coates House expanded. Its second-floor dining room installed indoor window shutters, and these, along with drapery, shielded patrons from street-level commotion. All the food was cooked to order and prepared in-house by a corps of chefs.[24] They relied on the railroad to ensure all manner of expensive delicacies. Dinners were lavish affairs that copied English Victorian dining protocols, best illustrated when President Grover Cleveland and his bride, Frances Folsom Cleveland, visited Kansas City in October 1887, after the hotel constructed an addition at the Eleventh Street corner. The meal began with chilled oysters, followed by turtle soup or consommé. Roast capon came next and then prime rib of roast beef with Yorkshire pudding, saddle of mutton and turkey with oyster stuffing. This preference for Anglo-American food continued through dessert, when apple, lemon and pumpkin pies were offered.[25]

Initially, Coates House faced little competition in the luxury dining category, but Kansas City's increasing reputation for hospitality ushered in numerous contenders. The downtown area shed some of its dirt and mayhem for paved streets, streetcar lines, department stores and newer hotels. To remain relevant, Coates House financed a remodel between 1889 and 1891.

Still in operation at the close of World War II, Coates House was by then a modest choice. Its profits were helped by its restaurant, operated by Harry Weiss (see chapter 9). Patrons feasted therein, but most were ignorant of

Coates House Hotel, interior view of the dining area. *Courtesy of Missouri Valley Special Collections, Kansas City Public Library (Kansas City, MO).*

the fact that the Coates House had once been travelers' best option for a luxurious meal and a stay in Kansas City.

By the 1970s, the Coates House was operated as tenement lodging, and Weiss had relocated to the Twin Oaks Apartment Complex. The grand old building came to a tragic end when, on January 28, 1978, a fire gutted its south side. The Historic Kansas City Foundation purchased the remaining structure to ensure it would not be razed, and in 1984, McCormack Baron Salazar Company rebuilt it. Since 2008, the structure has housed condominiums. Sadly, no restaurant draws in diners, but its storied past is integral to Kansas City's sense of its early culinary potential.

Hotel Baltimore

Hotel Baltimore became Kansas City's next grand hotel. When it was razed in 1939 to make room for a parking lot, Kansas Citians' regret was palpable. What made the Baltimore so special? Why was it publicly mourned? The answer rests with its reputation for some of the finest gourmet dining west of the Mississippi and two chefs who made it so.

Kansas City was lucky that Gustav F.M. Beraud was a swindler looking for a fresh start. He cooked in New York for the Astor family, but his skirmishes with the law left Beraud seeking a lower profile. He decided that Kansas City might offer him a new platform, and he became chef de cuisine at the Baltimore when it opened in 1899. David S. Shields wrote that Beraud "wished to generate public interest in good cooking." He took the then-novel approach of authoring a recipe column for the *Kansas City Star* aimed at women. He championed fresh ingredients and advised readers to limit their red meat intake—a bold move given the city's reputation for meatpacking. Recalibrated for home kitchens, Beraud's recipes taught cooks how to roast a chicken and make an old-fashioned hasty pudding with cornmeal and maple syrup. However, many recipes, including "lobster à la Newberg," brought Hotel Baltimore's luxury right into home kitchens. In the process, Beraud augmented Baltimore Hotel's reputation as a favorite dining destination, and his recipe column made him arguably Kansas City's first celebrity chef.[26]

When Beraud left the Baltimore in 1903, Adrian Delvaux replaced him. He, too, cultivated a following, but unlike Beraud, Delvaux had no scruples about promoting beef. Instead of confining his recipes and advice to the *Kansas City Star*, Delvaux reached a larger audience via Archie Hoff's 1913 *International Cooking Library*, likely convincing some readers to make Kansas City's Hotel Baltimore a destination in and of itself.

In 1908, the Baltimore expanded from a single unit on the southeast corner of Baltimore Avenue to take up a city block. In the process, it added new dining options. The huge central kitchen with an in-house refrigeration plant supplied food for the basement grill, main dining room, grand banquet hall, Automobile Room (with automobile murals), Egyptian Room Café (designed to "carry the diner back to the Egyptian period," with carved hieroglyphics on its columns) and elegant Pompeian Room, with white columns accented in red and green onyx. Advertisements in the society magazine *Independent* recommended the Pompeian Room as "a delightful climax to the afternoon or evening theatre party."[27]

Chef Delvaux piqued jaded taste buds with signature dishes, such as lobster Baltimore, sautéed with mushrooms, brandy, tomatoes and demi-glace; he also ensured that less-ambitious diners were treated to expertly prepared steaks. Delvaux capitalized on his location in a cattle market that was second only to the market in Chicago; he worked exclusively with "holiday-grade" cuts, industry speak for the highest quality.

Although Hotel Baltimore was a victim of the Great Depression and closed in 1938, it played a significant role in setting the highest culinary standards. In its heyday, it brought in visitors who simply wanted to taste the food that the chefs created for their delight.

Savoy Hotel and Grill

The Baltimore and most hotels of that era sported grill rooms, but in Kansas City, only one rose to iconic heights: the Savoy Grill in the Savoy Hotel. Until a fire consumed its kitchen in 2014, the Savoy Grill was Kansas City's oldest continuously operating restaurant, and throughout its more-than-a-century-long existence, it recalled the heyday of train travel, Pendergast-era politics and the three-martini lunch.

Initially called the Thorne Hotel, the Savoy Hotel was built in 1888 at Ninth and Central Streets. This five-story-tall accommodation catered to businessmen arriving at Union Depot. Four years later, the Thorne Hotel was sold to John Arbuckle and William Arbuckle Jamison, partners in the New York Arbuckle Coffee Company. It was reopened in 1894 as the Savoy Hotel. The grill was added when the hotel also built a sixth story. The grill's bar was beautiful, as were the Santa Fe Trail murals commissioned by Edward J. Holslag, the high-backed green leather booths with brass lanterns, oak-paneled walls and Art Deco stained-glass windows.[28]

The ragtime and cabaret craze likely pressured the Savoy Grill to relax its "men's only" policy. Nearby grill rooms were doing so, oftentimes attracting actresses (and their fans) in need of a beer and meal. The Savoy wisely followed suit, given that women inevitably enlivened the atmosphere, and a younger generation was eager to comingle without the Victorian prudishness of yesteryear interfering.[29]

The Savoy occasionally changed its menu to reflect new culinary trends and technology. Initially, wild game was featured. The chefs worked consistently, however, to best other restaurants in the quality of their seafood, first with oysters and then, as refrigeration and transportation technology improved, with live Atlantic lobsters, which they stored in a huge kitchen tank. Seafood brought the Savoy Grill its highest accolades, and indeed, many older Kansas Citians remember having their first lobster dinner at the Savoy.

The Savoy Grill was patronized by Kansas City's "movers and shakers." Tom Pendergast ensured the liquor supply to the Savoy Grill during

ONE OF THE TWELVE SANTA FE TRAIL MURALS BY EDWARD HOLSLAG

SAVOY GRILL — 9th and Central Sts. — KANSAS CITY, MO. 6A-H1707

A postcard depicting one of the Holslag murals that adorned the Savoy Grill. *Courtesy of Missouri Valley Special Collections, Kansas City Public Library (Kansas City, MO).*

Prohibition. A young Harry S. Truman first patronized the Savoy on lunch breaks while working as a haberdasher, ultimately becoming the grill's most famous patron. As president, Truman used his favorite booth, number 4, for everything from political lunches to evening dinners with his wife, Bess.

Critical to maintaining confidentiality were the Savoy waiters, who were identified by numbers on their brass badges. In his 2002 restaurant review, Charles Ferruzza noted that numbers 1 and 2 had been retired long ago. Number 1 belonged to Leiman Childs, who served from 1950 to 1975. Bill Bass wore badge number 2. He retired in 1972, after fifty-two years of service, and his reputation for his knowledge of seafood was undisputed.[30]

The Savoy's longtime owner Don Lee helped ensure that the grill and hotel were placed in the National Register of Historic Places in 1974. Nonetheless, business faltered—partly the result, recalled former waiter Jack Holland, of computers. Until their arrival, work was often carried out in-person at restaurants. Computers and, later, the internet made face-to-face negotiations too time-consuming, and people began to "eat lunch while working at their desks."[31]

The October 23, 2014 fire that destroyed the Savoy Grill resulted in a mourning period for Kansas City, so much so that in 2018, 21C Museum Hotels reopened the hotel and the "Savoy at 21C." While the old Savoy

Grill was modernized, the original 1906 dining room remains largely unchanged. In memory of the grill's reputation for its seafood and steak, Head Chef Joe West ensures that his seasonal menu pays homage to both.

TRAINS AND PLANES: DINING AT UNION STATION AND THE DOWNTOWN AIRPORT

Fred Harvey Union Station

The Savoy benefited largely from its proximity to Union Depot, but after the Flood of 1903, the new Union Station was built on higher ground, and with it came significant competition to hotel dining, thanks to the Fred Harvey Company.

According to the 1914 floor plan, Union Station fully participated in Kansas City's segregationist traditions; a basement waiting room for "immigrant or second-class" patrons included a segregated lunchroom counter, while the main floor of Harvey Lunchroom catered to everyone else. "Harvey Girls" were famous for serving patrons delicious food at fair prices. Many loved the full breakfast, with pancakes and maple syrup, steak and eggs, hash browns, apple pie and coffee. A 1949–50 dinner menu featured American favorites, all prepared at the highest standards. A hamburger was sold for $0.65, and a gratinéed, creamed, diced chicken and mushroom open-faced sandwich with a salad rang up for $1.50.[32]

While Harvey Girls worked the lunchroom, the Fred Harvey Restaurant initially hired only male waiters, and its cuisine was prepared by European chefs. In 1936, when the restaurant became the Westport Room, the front-of-house operations were overseen by Kansas City's beloved maître d' Joe Maciel. He recalled that era as one in which "great men measured their worth by their belt size"—chief among them was Tom Pendergast. Maciel described him to columnist Arthur S. Brisbane as a "big man, a very quiet man, and a hearty eater."[33]

With deep-piled red carpeting, red mohair cushioned benches and thick, plate-glass doors, the Westport Room and Cocktail Lounge muted station noise, creating an ambiance of calm glamor. Hildreth Meière murals depicted the storied past of Westport Landing while patrons feasted on fried red snapper cheeks, Shrimp Creole, aged steaks and prime rib.

World War II's conclusion brought significant changes to the Harvey restaurants. In 1957, the Lunchroom's ceilings were lowered to save on

Dinner at the Westport Room, circa the 1950s. *Photograph courtesy of Rick Moehring.*

heating, and its counter seating was removed. The Westport Room was remodeled, this time with the "'floating palace' elegance of the Mississippi riverboats" but with a "twentieth-century...restraint, functional quality and lush color," wrote a *Kansas Citian* reporter.[34] The murals were covered with what looked like riverboat windows so diners could fantasize about looking out on the Mississippi River's banks.

The cooking remained superb. At noon, Chef Martin Gierster carved roast beef for sandwiches, using knives that he had brought with him from Germany.[35] Joe Maciel continued to keep both patrons and waitstaff happy with his wit, attention to detail and generosity. He invented the Westport Room's famous chicken Maciel, prepared tableside and consisting of tender chicken chunks in a curry-sherry cream sauce served on top of saffron-stained rice.

Ultimately, the Lunchroom and the Westport Room ceased turning profits, and as Union Station's operations declined, the Fred Harvey Company closed them in 1968. The Westport Room's elegance and the Lunchroom's comfort food do persist in the city's memory, helped by frequent republications of recipes.

MILLEMAN-GILBERT AIRPORT RESTAURANT AND FOUR WINDS RESTAURANT

The decline of the Fred Harvey Company and Union Station was the inevitable result of planes replacing trains as the preferred mode of cross-country transportation. "Where famous sky travelers dine" was how Joe Gilbert characterized his concessions at the Municipal Downtown Airport. While the Four Winds Restaurant was synonymous with airplane glamour and still fondly recalled today, Gilbert began with the more modest Milleman-Gilbert—or Airport—Restaurant, which was opened in 1940 in the terminal building.

Gilbert had turned around one of his father-in-law's floundering Fowler's Lunch Counters, giving him the confidence to branch out. He contacted the city manager and bid on concessions at the airport. When Gilbert's offer was accepted, restaurateur Truman "True" Milleman, a former manager of the Fred Harvey Union Station Restaurants and the owner of Nance's Café, became Gilbert's partner.[36] Milleman brought Fred Harvey's wisdom that "good travel follows good food routes"; Gilbert brought his hospitality, welcoming patrons into the Restaurant with its Air-Vue Terrace, where patrons watched planes land and take off.

A postcard depicting Milleman-Gilbert Airport Restaurant, 1950. *Author's collection.*

When Milleman sold his share in the business, Gilbert ran it with his son J. William "Bill" Gilbert. In December 1958, the city council approved a new restaurant building where Gilbert's Airline Catering Company kitchen would be located (his company prepared in-flight meals for airlines), as well as Gilbert's new fashionable restaurant Four Winds that opened in 1964.[37]

By that point, the Gilberts and their partner, Paul Robinson, were operating Plaza III, Inn at the Landing and the Holiday Inn Restaurant near the airport. But when Four Winds opened, many said that this Gilbert-Robinson restaurant was their favorite due to its convenience when entertaining out-of-town guests and its ambiance. "Some of the excitement and romance of airplanes taking off and landing carr[ied] into the room," wrote columnist Dick Brown.[38]

While the airport's coffee shop, the Weathervane, resembled the Harvey Lunchroom in its efficient twenty-four-hour service, Four Winds resembled the Westport Room. Visitors reached it via an escalator and entered through imposing wooden doors, recalled Jay Huey, the son of Four Winds' late Executive Chef Marvin Carroll Huey Sr.[39] The space was intimate, with red-brown brick walls, wood paneling and red, green and yellow plaid carpet. The room was dominated by the charcoal broiler, where steaks and kebabs were grilled over hickory. There is no doubt that patrons requested seating close to its friendly warmth on winter nights.

Despite its romance and great food, the Four Winds was adversely affected when Kansas City International (KCI) opened for commercial service in 1972. Joe Gilbert put a good face on matters. Not only did he secure the concessions contract at KCI, but he also made the parking headache that locals endured when trying to eat at the Four Winds disappear. Gilbert trumpeted that fact in the November 1972 *Kansas City Times*, advertising free parking and birthday cake to celebrate thirty-two years of Joe Gilbert operations at the airport—but to no avail. By 1973, Four Winds had closed. Gilbert-Robinson Inc. would go on to grow its reputation as the city's most highly regarded restaurant group, but none of those restaurants recall the glamor and excitement that Four Winds brought to airport dining in Kansas City.

Two Ends of the Spectrum:
Muehlebach Hotel and Street Hotel

Muehlebach Plantation Grill and Terrace Grill

A strict Jim Crow sensibility meant that well into the 1950s, Black and White people could not dine in the same restaurants or sleep in the same hotels. While the notion of "separate but equal" was farcical, hoteliers in what is now Kansas City's Historic Eighteenth and Vine District still worked hard to offer Black patrons a semblance of the luxury that White patrons took for granted when it came to dining and accommodations. The model of what "luxury" entailed for White and Black patrons alike was the Muehlebach (now part of the downtown Marriott). A massive hotel, it housed numerous restaurants over the years, including when it opened in 1915 at Baltimore Avenue and Twelfth Street.

The Muehlebach's most notable eatery was Plantation Grill, the first restaurant in Kansas City to broadcast live music, via radio station WDAF, hence bringing Kansas City's "Paris of the plains" reputation to people as far away as Canada and Mexico. The story goes that in December 1922, Carlton A. Coon and Joe L. Sanders were finishing up their band's midnight program when Leo Fitzpatrick joked into a live mic that "anyone who'd stay up this late to hear us would have to be a real nighthawk!" The next week, five thousand listeners wrote to confirm that they were nighthawks, and the band added the term to its name, making it the Nighthawk Orchestra. Thousands were determined to travel to Kansas City to listen to that orchestra, dance and eat at the fabled Plantation Grill.[40]

The food reflected 1920s American taste. One satisfied patron kept his menu as a souvenir, marking dishes he wished to remember: Scotch mutton broth with barley, shrimp curry, garden tomatoes and peach shortcake with Chantilly cream. This dinner set him back $1.95, the equivalent of roughly $34.00 in 2021.

When the stock market crash jeopardized the Muehlebach's profits, it was sold in 1931 to the Trianon Hotel Company, which was then under the leadership of Kansas City's most famous hotelier, Barney Allis.[41] Due to his talents, the Muehlebach not only sustained its revenue, but it profited, becoming the city's leading hotel.

Allis transformed the Plantation Grill into the Terrace Grill, "so designated because two levels are being installed" to "provide better visibility and a more intimate atmosphere," noted a *Kansas City Star* reporter.[42] There, people

A postcard depicting Terrace Grill, postmarked 1940. *Author's collection.*

celebrated special occasions and customs, particularly during the Christmas season, when families dined while shopping downtown. Until its close in 1976, countless bands and crooners, from Guy Lombardo to Buddy Rogers, took the mic while WHB Radio broadcast the performances live, as WDAF had done previously.

Many big Kansas City hospitality names got their start in the Muehlebach kitchens, including hotelier Philip Pistilli, who began his career as a dishwasher. Chef Jess Barbosa, himself hired by Pistilli, climbed the ladder to become Muehlebach's executive chef by 1969. Barbosa infused the Muehlebach's menus with Spanish and Mexican flavors from his Kansas City Westside childhood, including his popular sopa de arroz, chicken mole and poached game hens in cilantro-jalapeño broth.[43]

Journalist Jess Ritter dated the Muehlebach's decline to 1962, when Allis sold his interest. When it was purchased by Radisson in 1976, no fine-dining restaurant ever matched the prestige of the Plantation or Terrace Grills. When Muehlebach was purchased in 1996 by Marriott, hotel fine-dining had largely disappeared, replaced by the chef-driven independent restaurants with eclectic menus discussed in chapter 5. Today, the Muehlebach continues to be used for banquets and receptions, but it no longer attracts Kansas Citians looking for the fantastic food, atmosphere and entertainment that made it the happening place for patrons from the 1920s through the 1960s.

Street Hotel

"Imagine what it would be like staying in a fine New York City hotel, like the Waldorf-Astoria, and coming down every morning to breakfast, nodding hello to Frank Sinatra or Doris Day or Fred Astaire as you pass by their tables," Buck O'Neil recalled. "Well, that's what it felt like for me… staying in the Streets Hotel at Eighteenth and Paseo and coming down to the dining room, where Cab Calloway and Billie Holiday and Bojangles Robinson often ate."[44] Indeed, the Street (or Streets) Hotel exemplified what Black entrepreneurial talent could accomplish in segregated Kansas City. With its famous Blue Room and Rose Room in operation from 1919 to 1960, the hotel was the most exclusive option for Black dining and entertainment.

Young Reuben Street settled with his family in Wyandotte County when they moved from Williamson County, Tennessee, in 1883.[45] After living in other cities along the Missouri River, Reuben and his wife, Ella, decided that the Black district in Kansas City, Missouri, would best support their culinary aspirations. After running a couple of small eateries, the couple settled in 1917 at 1510 East Eighteenth Street, opening Reuben's and Ella's Street Café. Success prompted them to apply for financial help from funeral home directors Theron B. and John Watkins and expand operations. They opened their hotel in 1919.[46]

At that point, their café became the Rose Room, a 125-seat à la carte restaurant. A *Kansas City Call* article marveled that the restaurant's tables and chairs were trimmed in fashionable chrome and that "costly window drapes and asphalt-tile flooring all match and blend with perfect harmony to make a refreshing atmosphere."[47] Chef de Cuisine John R. Ross Jr. oversaw the food, grilling patrons' steaks and chops to order, as well as preparing seafood that rivaled that of the Savoy Grill.[48]

The Blue Room was presided over by Jesse "Kingush" Fisher, Kansas City's first famous mixologist. Kansas City Jazz, a hard-swinging dance music indebted to the blues, came into being at the Blue Room, particularly after Count Basie joined the house band, Bennie Moten's Kansas City Orchestra, in 1929.[49] As the city's premier "black-and-tan" club, where the races were

Reuben Street in front of his hotel. *Courtesy of the Black Archives of Mid-America (Kansas City, MO).*

not subjected to explicit segregation, the Blue Room illustrated what could happen to creativity when people were not forced to understand their world through the lens of color.[50]

By the late 1940s, the Streets bought their hotel after twenty-eight years of leasing it.[51] In 1949, they gave their establishment a $250,000 facelift and purchased a glowing neon-pink sign "girding the Eighteenth Street and the Paseo Street side of the building," as reported the *Kansas City Call*.[52]

"I...get a bittersweet feeling because I remember that a lot of people lost their whole way of life [when legal segregation ended]," recalled Buck O'Neil. This social change resulted in "another one of those ironies, the hardest one," he continued. "Not only did a Black business die, other Black businesses did, too, the ones that were dependent on Black baseball and Black entertainment. The Streets Hotel had to close, because it couldn't compete with the Muehlebach downtown."[53]

Nevertheless, the Streets had made a comfortable living. After Ella's death in 1953, Reuben sold the hotel to Robert L. Williams and retired. While the

Rose Room was not re-created after the building was razed, the Blue Room was. It resides in the American Jazz Museum at 1616 East Eighteenth Street, where jazz still pulses into the wee hours of the morning and reminds people of a bittersweet time in Kansas City's culinary history.

THE SUNSET OF AN ERA:
THE ALAMEDA AND THE HYATT REGENCY

Alameda Rooftop and Pam Pam West

Oftentimes, the rooftop restaurants that were all the rage in the 1970s and '80s were about show—not quality. While Kansas City had its share of rooftop restaurants, they did not achieve fame for their great cuisine.

Alameda Rooftop was the exception. Gilbert-Robinson and hotelier Phil Pistilli ran the Alameda Hotel, but the rooftop restaurant's success is credited to Jess Barbosa. He followed Pistilli from the Muehlebach as the executive chef when the Alameda opened in 1971.

To complement the Spanish-Moorish architecture of the Country Club Plaza, the Rooftop restaurant incorporated "dark, heavy beams, high ceilings, and wrought-iron decorative accessories," wrote the authors of *Dining In: Kansas City*. "A symphony in orange," enthused reviewers Sylvia and Colin Clarendon. Iron chandeliers and marble columns rounded out the Rooftop's interior, with the menus decorated with the hotel's adaptation of the Papal Seal.[54] The dark interior worked beautifully with huge windows that allowed natural light to come in. Diners seated on the north looked down on the Plaza, while those on the south looked out toward Loose Park. Evenings were rendered seductively intimate with candlelight, and reservations were made months in advance to capture a prime seat during the holiday season, when the Plaza was ablaze in lights. Deborah Bowman remembered that the line to enter the Rooftop to see the Plaza lights was so long that "waitstaff took drink orders."[55]

The food was superior. Paupiettes of Sole Santa Maria earned Barbosa a first-place award from the Missouri Restaurant Association, and that dish joined other distinctive offerings, including seasonal gazpacho, escallops of veal in morel mushroom cream sauce and quivering flans with fresh raspberries.

Meanwhile, Pam Pam West, the Alameda's coffee shop, was filled with "tuxes and bikers and omelets at 2:00 a.m.," remembered Fred Grunwald.

"Locals loved it," wrote Shifra Stein, for its convenience, comfortable atmosphere and high-quality food."[56] Breakfast was served all day, and the "hangover omelet," with its kick of green chili, was a hit. Children adored the tin roof sundae, with vanilla ice cream covered in hot fudge, English toffee crumbs and toasted almonds. Pam Pam's coffee was rich and strong. Stein enthused, "Waitresses will oblige you by filling up your cup as many times as you wish." The Pam Pam potato burger was a favorite after burning calories dancing in the Rooftop lounge. A hollowed-out baked potato was stuffed with ground beef, spices, minced onions, Parmesan cheese and sour cream, topped with cheddar and rebaked until it became a glistening, gooey wonder of carbs and protein.

The Alameda's demise resulted from a joint venture between Ritz-Carlton Hotels and J.C. Nichols Company. Nichols's president Lynn McCarthy "no longer considered it a jewel on the company's balance sheet," wrote the *Kansas City Business Journal*. Despite its reputation, the hotel had lost money, leading Nichols to sell it to Ritz-Carlton in 1988. "Nothing will ever replace the Phil Pistilli days at the Alameda," wrote longtime patron Kurt Fahey. "Nothing has been the same since." We will let Fahey have the last word.[57]

Hyatt Regency's Peppercorn Duck Club

The Peppercorn Duck Club likewise basks in the glow of nostalgia, the last of Kansas City's twentieth-century fine hotel restaurants. During its heyday, the Duck Club, as it was known, excelled in all respects. It offered crave-worthy food, attentive service and an ambiance so all-embracing that when the check was presented alongside the complementary chocolate-dipped strawberries and red roses, a "Darn it, we're worth it!" response was more likely than a gasp at the price. By 1980, most of the area's remaining hotel restaurants could not hit all the notes in the chord quite like the Duck Club.

The Hyatt Regency opened in August 1980, with the Duck Club located on the second floor off the escalator. The spotlights danced off the restaurant's brass trim and copper rotisserie, offering an intimate contrast to the airy greenhouse feel of the Hyatt lobby below. Tapestry-upholstered banquettes beckoned diners to genuinely relax and allow the evening to unfold while harp music played in the distance. Meanwhile, diners gazed at the sunken, multiservice table that included the Ultra Chocolatta Bar, "devoted to gastronomic lasciviousness such as is rarely seen in these parts," marveled reporter Jonathan Probber.[58]

It was, after all, the 1980s. Indulgence and go-go-optimism created the zeitgeist embodied in the Chocolatta Bar's display of "jewel-like confections," including flourless chocolate "sin cake." Devised by Chef Dwight Byers, it sat temptingly among Byers's forest of edible chocolate branches and flowers.[59]

"It wasn't just the food," insisted Charles Broomfield. "It was the *aroma* of the food. My gosh, I remember stepping off the escalator to the smell of that grilled garlic bread!"[60] The aroma harmonized with the fragrance of roast duckling stuffed with apples and oranges and rubbed with rosemary, fennel and star anise. The bird arrived at the table to be finished in the sauce of one's choice, from peppercorn to kumquat.

The Duck Club did face significant challenges, however. At 7:05 p.m., on July 19, 1981, the fourth-floor skywalk split and spilled down onto the second-level skywalk, which also collapsed; 114 people died, and over 200 were injured in the disaster. The Duck Club's and the Hyatt's ability to recover was far from assured. When they both reopened on October 2, "no one wept," but "no one forgot," wrote reporter Rick Atkinson. There was "no smug self-congratulation or lugubrious mourning but simply a low-key attempt to turn a mausoleum back into a hotel."[61] That low-key attitude did help the city heal, and by the mid-1980s, the Duck Club was again "a see-and-be-seen place." "Everyone went there," recalled an employee when speaking to Charles Ferruzza.[62] Reservations ran three weeks out, while Valentine's Day was booked months in advance.

For obscure reasons, the Duck Club was not remodeled to keep up with the times, and by 2000, the brass and upholstery were stuck in a time warp. The food remained delicious, but the Duck Club became pigeonholed as "grandma's favorite special occasion restaurant," not the choice of younger, fashionable diners. Ferruzza speculated that at least some of the Duck Club's demise rested with the Hyatt, which was working to "gently" ease "the classic dining room out of the picture permanently." Writing in May 2010, Ferruzza rightly sensed that the restaurant's end was near—so, too, was the end of almost two centuries of Kansas City hotel fine dining.

3
Motoring to Dinner

BYWAY AND HIGHWAY EATERIES

As the automobile displaced public transportation, the United States underwent a highway-building boom. Eateries popped up to cater to motorists, particularly roadside teahouses and drive-ins. Another factor played a role in the proliferation of roadside eateries: the passage of the Eighteenth and Nineteenth Amendments. As Jan Whitaker points out in *Tea at the Blue Lantern Inn: A Social History of the Tea Room Craze in America* (2002), the automobile became popular around the time that Prohibition came into force and as women won the right to vote. While fancy restaurants were adversely affected by Prohibition, newly enfranchised women seized the opportunity to open teahouses and inns that served homey food that was best accompanied by iced tea or coffee—not wine or spirits. Meanwhile, teenagers awash in postwar prosperity made the drive-in their haunt. Let's experience an era that celebrated women's entrepreneurship, the automobile and baby boomers' rites of passage by traveling back to some of Kansas City's roadside eateries.

GREEN PARROT INN

Writing about Tena May Dowd's Green Parrot Inn in 1945, WHB's *Swing* described it as "one of the nicer excuses for taking a little drive. Mrs. Dowd maintains an establishment of real quality, with excellent food served skillfully in a gracious atmosphere. Three large dining rooms are softly dressed, linens and silver are company best."[63] Located at Fifty-Second Street and State Line Road in Shawnee Mission, Kansas, the Green Parrot continued the standard of serving fried chicken dinners that the Harris House had excelled with and that many of us still enjoy today.

Dowd endorsed the dictates of good food set forth by Duncan Hines in *Adventures in Good Eating*, promising customers from-scratch cooking, with a focus on seasonal foods. She initially opened a restaurant in Wichita, but her husband's transfer to Kansas City led the Dowds to purchase a weedy seven acres on the Kansas side of the state line to build the Green Parrot. A prominent supporter of a "dry Kansas," Dowd liked to tell the story of how the realtors reacted with disbelief when she told them that she planned to run a fancy inn that did not serve alcohol.[64]

After opening in 1929, the Green Parrot accommodated diners on its terraces and in "dining rooms which overlook two states from atop a hill," read a postcard. Guests sat down to fried chicken, the most popular meal, but they could also opt for chicken pie, turkey and dressing or lamb chops, among other choices. Its desserts were famous, with strawberry shortcake a springtime favorite.

Memories of the Green Parrot center on important life events. In the 1930s and '40s, an excursion there required planning and money, as well

Our Specialty - Fried Chicken Dinners

GREEN PARROT INN - 52nd St. and State Line - Kansas City, Mo.

A postcard depicting Green Parrot Inn, located at Fifty-Second Street and State Line Road. *Courtesy of Missouri Valley Special Collections, Kansas City Public Library (Kansas City, MO).*

as a justification to splurge, given the Depression and then World War II rationing. A message scrawled across a Green Parrot postcard is illustrative: "Dear Folks, This is where Loren Jr. and Helen took Dad for his birthday. We really had a very nice [time] etc."

Dowd helped shape a nationwide movement to promote "Mother's home cooking" at restaurants away from Mother's home. Her hard work, hospitality and professional networking resulted in her success not only in Kansas City but in opening a Green Parrot Inn with her brother J.H. Toothman in Kirkwood, Missouri, in 1936 (it closed in 1983) and another with her sister Vera Fredericks in Houston in 1952 (it closed in 1967). Kansas City's Green Parrot closed in 1955. If Kansas City sometimes claims the fried chicken dinner as its own contribution to American good eats, that claim rests largely with Dowd's efforts and her definition of wholesome food made better with a tall glass of iced tea.

STEPHENSON'S APPLE FARM AND RESTAURANT

Although most roadside inns were the result of the hard work of women entrepreneurs during this era, Stephenson's was the brainchild of twin brothers Loyd and Les. However, women were still integral to their success, as Loyd explained to Boots Mathews and James Rieger, because "the woman decides where to go eat….She's got to like it. We've got to romance the women."[65] Former first lady Bess Truman was so romanced that she sometimes hosted her bridge club at the restaurant.[66]

Les and Loyd joined thousands of World War II veterans who had to figure out how to make a livelihood. They started a luncheonette on their family farm off 40 Highway and Lee's Summit Road, hoping smoked meat sandwiches and cider might bring in more business than a produce stand.[67] Indeed, the luncheonette became popular, so the brothers opened a restaurant specializing in smoked meat and many apple dishes and drinks. But when it came to attracting women patrons, the brothers worked hardest on the restaurant's interiors, creating, as Mathews and Rieger judged, "one of the first atmosphere restaurants in town."

Kansas City Chef Jasper Mirable recalled his parents taking the family to dinner there: "I remember walking into the Parlour, the first room to the left of the lobby, red-velvet wallpaper and a little faux balcony, one of eight dining rooms….I remember the paintings on the wall, the white tablecloths, starched napkins, candles on each table and the big glasses."[68]

The Parlour was elegant, while the Cupboard Room made diners feel like they were eating in a farmhouse kitchen. The patio offered soft lighting by the glow of candles.

The restaurant's smoked brisket rivaled the brisket served at barbecue restaurants. The baked chicken in butter and cream, accompanied by green rice casserole, was arguably the restaurant's most popular meal. The apple fritters were also beloved, and if people still had room for dessert, they inevitably turned to the restaurant's apple dumplings. Many adults started their meals with frozen apple daiquiris.

Until the restaurant's closing in 2007, when the brothers were in their eighties, many people paid their bill and purchased *Stephenson's Restaurants Receipts* so they could make their own versions of their favorite dishes. When someone reminisces about Stephenson's on social media, it's only a matter of minutes before the green rice recipe makes its appearance, with its mounds of parsley, cream and cheddar cheese. In this way, memories of Les and Loyd and their contributions to Kansas City's culinary tapestry remain alive today.

WISHBONE RESTAURANT

World War II veteran Phillip A. Sollomi Sr. moved to Kansas City from Cleveland, Ohio, and invested "with a friend in a cocktail lounge," wrote reporter Victoria Sizemore Long. While information on that venture is obscure, by 1949, Sollomi had purchased a mansion on the corner of Forty-Fifth and Main Streets and opened the Wishbone Restaurant. Shortly thereafter, customers were clamoring for his dressing, a spicy vinaigrette whose recipe came from Sollomi's Sicilian-born mother, Lena.[69] Requests for it sent Sollomi out back to mix it in a fifty-gallon drum, and by 1952, Sollomi sold the restaurant to Joe and Dora Adelman to turn his attention to salad dressing.

The Adelmans, Kansas City's restaurant power couple, knew Kansas Citians took fried chicken seriously. Given the popularity of automobiles, they shrewdly invested in drive-ins (Rugel's), suburban family restaurants (the Drumstick) and their destination restaurant, the Wishbone, the one most firmly embedded in the city's culinary DNA.

The Adelmans' success resulted from ceaseless labor, with family members working the front and back of the house. Jackie Freedman recalled her mother's sheer tenacity and uncomplaining attitude. "She'd

A view of the front-facing exterior and driveway of the Wishbone Restaurant, 1952. *Courtesy of Missouri Valley Special Collections, Kansas City Public Library (Kansas City, MO).*

be up front, seating people. Mother's Day, Easter, and Thanksgiving." Only a week after such occasions would the family be able to enjoy a meal out themselves.[70]

The restaurant's size added to its appeal, with dining rooms for all occasions. But each one was outfitted with sparkling crystal and silver. Many children remembered birthday dinners in the Wishing Well Room, "with a very large stone wishing well in the middle of it," recalled Mary Accurso Dodd. First came a birthday cake with a lit sparkler, and on the way out, the birthday child received a shiny new penny to drop into the well.[71]

By the mid-1970s, the Adelmans were slowing down. They sold the restaurant to Stan Glazer, who, for a short time, ran the restaurant as Stanford's East and then as Outlaws. Both were gone by 1981. The mansion was razed, Main Street was regraded and all evidence of what had once been a sprawling driveway leading to a restaurant where families anticipated dinner and hospitality was obliterated.

OLD GRINTER HOUSE TEA ROOM

"The woman stood in the road and looked long and thoughtfully at the old red-brick house. Weeds in the yard were standing high, the windows boarded up, bricks falling out. 'Let's buy that lovely old place,' she said to her husband, 'I'll make it into a tearoom.'" Reporter Eleanor Richey Johnston related the story after Bernice and Harry Hanson bought the property at 1420 South Seventy-Eighth Street in Kansas City, Kansas.[72]

The Grinter estate was built by Moses and Annie Marshall Grinter to serve Santa Fe traders and the Lenape (Delaware) tribe, of which Annie was a member.[73] To return the house to its former beauty, the Hansons worked for eleven months, equipping the house for family-style dinners, luncheons and teas. As Bernice explained to her neighbors, "We want to share [the house] with everyone. The only way we can do this is to make the old house help pay its way."[74]

The restaurant opened in 1951, and its popularity led Bernice and Johnston to publish *The Old Grinter House Cook Book*. "Imagine as you eat fried chicken in these rooms of thick walls, high ceilings and fireplaces galore, the creaking ox carts that, in 1857, hauled the lumber needed for its building all the way from Fort Leavenworth," the authors wrote.[75]

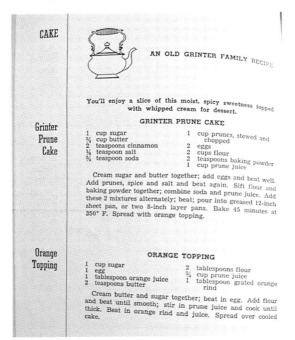

Grinter House's prune cake recipe. *From Eleanor Richey Johnston and Bernice Hanson,* Old Grinter House Cookbook *(place of publication: Grinter Place State Historical Society, 1953).*

The Tea Room catered to bridge clubs and civic groups, showcasing chicken timbales, fruit salads and popovers. In the evening, it offered specials, such as fried chicken and stuffed round steak, served with corn fritters and cucumber salad—homey food that made diners nostalgic for Grandmother's cooking. Most popular during winter, due to its warm, cinnamon-filled undertones, was the Hanson family prune cake. Imagine prunes reconstituted to become so unctuously soft that they disintegrate into the batter. The cake was covered with icing redolent of oranges. That brightness, combined with the cake's earthy sweetness, made Grinter Place popular for teatime and dessert.

In 1966, the Hansons were ready to retire but wanted their property preserved and protected. They closed the restaurant for regular business and devoted their time to educating the state about Grinter Place's significance. The State of Kansas acquired the estate in 1971, the year the house was placed in the National Register of Historic Places. The Hansons' dedication to restoring the property laid the foundation for the success of Grinter Place today, and it helped cement Kansas City's continued reputation for expertly prepared country-style cuisine.

Sandy's Oak Ridge Manor Tea House

When Louise and Darwin Sandstrom purchased the rambling estate at 5410 Northeast Oak Ridge Drive in 1954, their motivations resembled those of the Hansons, in that they, too, wished to preserve their county's pioneer heritage. Transforming Oak Ridge into a teahouse was the best way to do this.

The land was granted to David Hale in 1827. In 1840, Dr. James and Mary Ann Compton purchased it, and with the work of enslaved people, they cleared the land, farmed it and built a ten-room home around—and including—the Hales' two original cabins. They named their farm Oak Ridge.[76] With few roads and services present in that area, visitors counted on the family for food and rest. When Emma Compton, the last surviving family member, sold Oak Ridge to the Sandstroms, we can imagine that she was pleased that her family's reputation for hospitality would endure.

With no electricity or running water, the Sandstroms first modernized the property but "without changing its authenticity and pioneer flavor," Louise explained.[77] The original cabins were used for banquets and parties, while the Sandstroms added a larger dining room with windows overlooking the property.[78]

Sandy's Oak Ridge Manor, partial frontal view, 1993. *Courtesy of Missouri Valley Special Collections, Kansas City Public Library (Kansas City, MO).*

After Darwin passed away in 1959, Louise operated the restaurant on her own. As she aged, Louise left the kitchen duties to her cooks and became the hostess. At four feet, six inches tall, Louise was just right for the small frame of the restaurant's front door, through which tall customers had to stoop to enter. Often, Louise's Great Dane was nearby to greet visitors, too.

Many crossed town to partake in the house's specialty: sauerbraten with potato pancakes and honey-buttered carrots and turnips. As was customary at family-style restaurants, the main course was preceded by the option of a salad (Sandy's was served with a sweet-tart pink dressing) or chicken noodle soup. The peanut butter pie for dessert was also praised.

By the early 1980s, Louise had worked in hospitality most of her life, first as cook in her and Darwin's North Kansas City tavern and then at Sandy's. She was ready to retire. The estate passed to brothers Mike and Dennis Donegan and Jim Hogan, who had recently saved Helen Stroud's fried chicken roadhouse (see chapter 10). They needed a second location to meet their demand, and it made sense to buy Sandy's, given its family-style service model and surroundings. So, Oak Ridge Manor lives on robustly today, albeit as Stroud's Oak Ridge Manor, or Stroud's North for short.

Peter's Drive-In and Mrs. Peter's Chicken Dinners

John E. and Bernadine C. Peter created an iconic drive-in and a fried chicken restaurant; yet, when these establishments closed, the couple responsible for so many fond memories of diners in Kansas City, Kansas, seemed to vanish. Let's resurrect their story. The couple moved to Kansas City, Kansas, in 1945 and operated an ice cream vending service before opening one of the state's first Zesto Drive-Ins at Twenty-Ninth Street and Minnesota Avenue. Shortly thereafter, they moved to 3212 State Avenue, eventually dropped the Zesto franchise and became Peter's Drive-In.[79]

State Avenue was a major thoroughfare—or perhaps we might say drag strip—awash at night with neon and headlights. Former Peter's Drive-In fan Cait McKnelly brings the scene back to life: "Saturday nights saw teens from Turner, Wyandotte, Washington and Sumner High Schools cruise up and down State Avenue, showing off their souped-up cars and occasionally getting into drag races. It was like a scene out of *Grease* every weekend."[80]

John and Bernadine ensured that their food would also share the spotlight with all the hotrods. The salad burger was their best seller. It was not "just a hamburger," with a limp slice of sorry tomato and wilted lettuce; rather, it was a virtual fresh salad on top of a thin meat patty, mixed with a creamy salad dressing. Bernadine also poured her heart into all manner of from-scratch goodies, chief among them her fried chicken dinners. Their popularity motivated Bernadine to start Mrs. Peter's Chicken Dinners at 4960 State Avenue in 1977, after John passed away. She sold the drive-in to longtime manager Arnold Jamison Jr., who kept it going until 1989. Meanwhile, Bernadine created a Kansas City, Kansas, version of Stroud's.[81]

The meals were simple. Most opted for fried chicken, but breaded pork chops, fried catfish and country fried steak were also on the menu, alongside coleslaw, a marinated vegetable salad, mashed potatoes and gravy, green beans and biscuits, followed by peach cobbler. This author can still taste the biscuits and indescribably delicious seasoning that graced the fried chicken.

The consistency of its food, hospitality and cheerful yellow interior, replete with folksy chicken art, made Mrs. Peter's a nationally recognized restaurant. Jane and Michael Stern's popular *Road Food* praised it, as did journalists who were writing it up in newspapers and magazines such as *Country Living*. Out-of-state license plates filled the parking spots not taken up by locals.

Eventually, age caught up with Bernadine. She sold the restaurant in 1982 to Ray T. "Tom" and Alice "Nadine" Baker. As with the Peters, the Baker family operated the restaurant with the same exacting standards.[82]

Mrs. Peter's remained the place to go for special-occasion dinners, holiday celebrations and business luncheons. But as quietly as it all began, the restaurant abruptly closed in 2000, to the dismay of thousands of fans. It and Peter's Drive-In are among Kansas City, Kansas's culinary icons, and they are arguably the most missed. But the legacies of both have remained surprisingly unsung.

ALLEN'S AND SMAKS

Allen's Drive-In was famous for the "Royal": "two steak burger patties, melted cheese, toasted triple bun, lettuce, and our own special dressing," read the menu. Wesley T. Fielder explained that his father and grandfather "copied Winstead's burger special—with Gordon Montgomery's blessing," Fielder assured.[83] (See chapter 10.) Allen's cooks pressed the burgers shoe-sole thin before sliding them hot off the grill and onto the toasted buns.

The Royal burger had ties to the American Royal. Every year, Caterers Inc., the company that Allen's became, purchased the first-place Herford at the American Royal to auction off for charity while giving its premier burger a name that Kansas Citians immediately identified with. Patricia Jones recalled that not long before Allen's closed, she "was pregnant and craving the Allen's Royal….I bought four the last day of business and froze them. Best burger in town."[84]

Let's go back to 1944, when Wayne Jones and his son-in-law William Otis "Bill" Fielder bought a boarded-up restaurant known as Allen's at Sixty-Third Street and The Paseo Boulevard. With their "shoestring budget," Bill and Wayne could not afford a new sign, so they kept the old one.[85] Within twenty years, Caterer's Inc. was born, and several Allen's Drive-Ins dotted the area. Recalling her childhood in Kansas City, Kansas, Julie Haas wrote, "We rarely went to a restaurant, but when we did, it was Allen's." Haas's favorite meal, the frankfurter, was described in a 1949 *Swing* magazine as "honestly…the most beautiful frankfurters you've ever seen. They're barbecued and they're thick, fat, juicy, tender and strictly palatable."[86]

By the time that Jones's other son-in-law, Ted Llewellyn, joined the company in 1954, Caterers Inc. was ready to expand in a new direction—fast food. While vacationing in San Bernardino in 1954, Fielder and Jones visited Richard and Maurice McDonald's burger shop to do some research.[87] Combining what they learned there with Fielder's fond memories of working at Smack, a Miami restaurant, Kansas City's own Smaks was born,

Smaks advertisements, 1975. *Author's collection.*

debuting in 1954 in Mission, Kansas, and spreading across and beyond the metro area.[88] Speed differentiated Allen's and Smaks, with Smaks using a counter service that was faster than curb service. To further add to the restaurant's appeal, advertisement executive Bill Witcher created Smaky, a seal puppet who granted his "seal of approval" to Smaks menu items, including a children's "Smaky Meal," with a burger, fries, a soft drink and a toy.[89] Sound familiar?

McDonald's—by then a powerful franchise—took notice and approached Caterers Inc. with an offer to let it control any new McDonald's that came to Missouri. The intention was to fold Smaks into McDonald's. The offer was refused. "We were family-owned," Wesley T. Fielder flatly explained. "Caterers Inc. didn't work fifteen years to become franchisees, let alone give up their name." Due most likely to the success of the Smaky Meal, McDonald's, in 1967, hired Bernstein-Rein Advertising in Kansas City to create its own child-targeted promotions, including the Happy Meal, which was test marketed in Kansas City and elsewhere in 1977.[90]

Nonetheless, the advertising power of national franchises like McDonald's spelled an end to many local drive-ins. By June 1978, Allen's at 8901 State Line Road, the sole survivor of the venerable chain, closed.[91] By 1986, all Smaks in the metro area had closed. Today, Smaky lives on in our memories, while Allen's will always be remembered as a rite of passage for thousands of teens with their new drivers' licenses and keys to the car.

SIDNEY'S DRIVE-IN

Kansas City, Missouri's "hot-rod loop" was anchored by Allen's and Sidney's. But Sidney Ginsberg and his brothers did not start with drive-ins. Instead, they started with twenty-four-hour restaurants, the longest lasting of which resided at 3623 Broadway Boulevard. Sidney's Inc. built its first drive-in in 1957 at Linwood Boulevard and Gillham Plaza. By 1959, Sidney's had also taken over a drive-in at Main Street and Ward Parkway in a building that was already considered a drive-in icon. Designed in a Wayne McAllister style, with a circular shape and giant neon pylon, the building had been the Forum Drive-In in 1941, then Z-Lan, Nu-Way and Y Drive-Ins afterward.[92]

Sidney's was famous for the "Big Buster," described on the menu as "two juicy hamburger patties with melted cheese, tasty relish spread and served on our sesame bun." In June 1965, *Esquire* featured an article on teenagers, noting that the Big Buster is "the favorite food of Kansas City youngsters."[93]

The food's quality was assured, because Sidney and his wife, Elizabeth, leased a 320-acre property south of Olathe to raise cattle and grow produce for use in the restaurants. The company routinely purchased American Royal prize-winning steers for the same reason: to ensure top quality.[94]

Not everyone went to Sydney's for the food. Sydney's went down in Kansas City restaurant history as the place to "buzz"—as in "buzz in and buzz out." The parking lots grew so congested that managers charged twenty-five cents per car, money that could be put toward a food order if the cruisers actually decided to stay and eat anything. "We'd spend most of the night driving between the Linwood Sidney's and the Plaza Sidney's," recalled Alexis Harmon. "Sit at one location, watch the muscle cars parade past, then drive to the other one and do the same thing. Maybe buy a hamburger or coke."[95]

Sensing a shift in dining trends, as teens sporting hotrods and drinking Cokes transformed into couples more prone to a date over cocktails, Sidney's Inc. transformed the 3150 Gillham Plaza drive-in into the Snooty Fox Restaurant and Cocktail Lounge in 1973. Meanwhile, the Main Street and Ward Parkway Sidney's buzzed for a few years longer. Joyce Bennett Schuyler recalled how "the guy with the loudest pipes and muffler on his car had to drag through" the lot, and when he stayed to order "into the sound system…it would get garbled, and everybody in the car would break up laughing.…It was the big thing to come to Sidney's," until suddenly, it was gone.[96] What had been one of Kansas City's most distinctive architectural structures and home to a series of highly regarded drive-ins was razed by the J.C. Nichols Company to make room for office and retail space.

4
Barbecue and Steakhouses

KANSAS CITY STYLE

Locally owned barbecue joints and steakhouses that reached iconic status laid culinary foundations that persist today. Many Kansas City restaurants offered steak or barbecue, but they did not self-consciously promote this. Those that did respected local tastes and Kansas City's stockyard heritage. They retained the city's distinctiveness and quirky individuality, and as such, they became beloved favorites. Let's relive their days by moving through a smoky haze, punctuated by the sounds of music, dancing, laughing and eating.

BARBECUE ROYALS:
HENRY PERRY, JOHNNY THOMAS, ARTHUR PINKARD, OTIS BOYD, GRACE HARRIS AND EARL QUICK

Barbecue, traditionally the stuff of celebrations and leisure, was, for centuries, the responsibility of Black men, first as enslaved men and then as freed men. When at their leisure, Black communities likewise barbecued as a means of deriving pleasure and relaxation, smoking a bit of this or that. Seldom was it about profit or even business. But things were about to change.

Henry Perry

What makes Kansas City's barbecue heritage distinct is Henry Perry. He operated stands from as early as 1908 to 1940, upending tradition by deciding to make a substantial living selling his barbecue. While he was surely not the first to attempt it, he was the most successful. And in the process of selling his barbecue, he not only brought up apprentices in his style, but he also generated hundreds of imitators who thought that if Perry could profit off selling smoked meat, they could, too.

Perry was born in Shelby County, Tennessee, and arrived in Kansas City in 1907. There, he worked as a saloon porter and in other jobs while also selling barbecue in the Garment District.[97] He also pitched a tent, dug a pit at Eighteenth and Vine Streets and sold his wares from there. By 1911, he was attracting attention, garnering a visit from a *Kansas City Star* reporter who spread the word of his barbecue farther.[98] How Perry received the title of "king" is obscure. He was the consummate marketer of his product, proud of his skill and popularity, and he probably styled himself as a "king" to promote his barbecue over his competitors. However, Perry's own account of a Kentucky senator bestowing that title on him "between mint juleps at a picnic" is likewise believable.[99] At any rate, the title stuck and remains today.

By 1911–12, Perry had built a stand at 1514 East Nineteenth Street on the north side of the street, between Vine Street and Highland Avenue.[100] "At that time," local historian Sonny Gibson explained, "Nineteenth and Highland was a dead end, but right above was the railroad track. Perry got a lot of his meat tossed down to him from the trains." Packinghouses discarded ribs, brisket and offal that was too poor to bother with, so it went for free or near it.[101] Perry let nothing go to waste. "I've never seen the meat yet I couldn't barbecue," he told the *Kansas City Star* reporter. "That goes for sheep, hogs, geese, chickens, fish, rabbits, squirrels, 'possums, oysters."

When asked what made his barbecue addictive, Perry had various answers. Most "mutts" are too "hot-headed," he told the *Kansas City Star* reporter. "They get in too big a hurry. I just baste and let the ground do the cooking." He also claimed he had a "special way" with barbecue. "Cooking over only a fire made with hickory and oak woods, the meat gets that delicious flavor." His fiery, vinegary sauce likewise stood out—it "so tickles the palate that they come back again and again for more," observed a *Kansas City Call* reporter.[102]

Perry expanded his operations, but of course, he was not operating by himself; his apprentices learned Perry's techniques before starting their own businesses. When Perry suffered a stroke in 1931, he relied heavily on former apprentice Charlie Bryant for help. That same year Arthur, Charlie's younger brother, decided to remain in Kansas City rather than return home to East Texas, and he, too, became Perry's apprentice. When Perry passed away in 1940, he left his 1921 East Eighteenth Street stand to Charlie Bryant (discussed in chapter 10).[103] Another Perry apprentice, Arthur Pinkard, became the pitman at Johnny Thomas's Ol' Kentuck Bar-B-Q (sometimes called Kentucky Barbecue) at 1516–18 East Nineteenth Street.

Johnny Thomas

Ol' Kentuck was a "pig iron" house, as saxophonist Henry "Buster" Smith called joints where "pork was served, liquor was drunk, and the bands played the blues all night in the keys of B, D, and E."[104] Patrons danced and refueled with barbecue and booze until the wee morning hours. Thomas catered to less-established musicians by offering them drums, a piano and ten-cent "barbecue soup" made of barbecue scraps.[105] Satisfied musicians made music, drawing in passersby. Who could resist the bebop when it was accompanied by the aroma of hickory and brisket? Key to the aroma was Pinkard, but he never drew fanfare to himself, so he remains obscure. Likewise significant to Kansas City's barbecue legacy was Pinkard teaching George and Arzelia Gates what he knew about barbecue (see chapter 10).

Otis P. Boyd

Perry settled in Kansas City, likely because he knew that its southern culinary roots promised citizens who recognized great barbecue—and who would be willing to pay for it. Perhaps Iowa native Otis P. Boyd was similarly motivated. After sizing up the hierarchy, he shrewdly avoided provoking fights with the likes of the Bryant brothers or George and Arzelia Gates; instead, he simply assumed he was part of a triumvirate. "Charlie Bryant, me [Boyd], and Gates was the ones that made Kansas City the barbecue capital of the United States.…Hell, I go up against any guy in the United States that *thinks* he can barbecue," Boyd told Eric Elie Lolis in 1995.[106]

Boyd created his own mythology, one that brought him accolades as food writers visited Kansas City to sample his mutton, hot links and sauce. Those items set Boyd apart from most of the competition, given that by the 1980s, when Boyd was thriving, mutton and hot links had largely disappeared from most Kansas City menus, and the flavors took people back to the days of Johnny Thomas and Henry Perry. As for the sauce, it's "90 percent of your barbecue," Boyd insisted to *Saveur*'s Connie McCabe. "Anybody can smoke some meat, as long as they get it done," he derisively said of his competition.[107]

Boyd began his career in Kansas City with a soul food and barbecue restaurant on the corner of Twelfth and Vine Streets, but most remember Boyd-N-Son Barbecue at 5510 Prospect Street that opened in 1967.[108] Boyd perfected his product more than he marketed it, toiling "in relative obscurity," observed Lolis.[109] Locals loved his barbecue, however, and Boyd trusted that outsiders who visited would appreciate his talent. They did—and so did his teenage waitress, Grace Lee Washington, who was interested in how her boss smoked meat.

Amazin' Grace Harris

A teenaged Grace moved from New Orleans to Kansas City, Kansas, with her family. While working for Boyd, she also absorbed the blues at her grandfather's nightclub and decided "that music was always going to be a part" of her life, even though her God-given gift, she explained, was to cook. So, she combined the two.[110] By the 1970s, she owned H&M Bar-B-Q at 1715 North Thirteenth Street in Kansas City, Kansas, where, until they heard "the rooster crow" and the dogs "barkin' at the sun," musicians played the blues and Grace served barbecue and Creole specials.[111] H&M literally kept Kansas City's "Paris of the plains" reputation alive—at least for those in the know. As with Boyd, "Amazin' Grace," as the musicians styled her, did little to publicize her juke joint.

People who cared learned quickly enough, especially Roger Naber, who opened the Grand Emporium in 1985 at 3832 Main Street. He wanted to create "an environment where Kansas City's own style of music and food would thrive," he explained to Doug Worgul, and the key to this was Harris. "The kind of music we wanted to feature here—blues, roots rock, jazz—it all just fits with barbecue," Naber explained."[112] Harris agreed to run Grand Emporium's kitchen, while, afterhours, she also ran H&M.

Harris was, as blues musician Glenn Patrik noted, "all action, no words."[113] She spoke through the flavors of her food. Harris's affinity with and affection for hungry musicians was repaid when they immortalized her in songs and memories, including Patrik's "Down to the Bar BQ" on *Original Blues*. "Ms.

Grace didn't charge musicians (although we weren't supposed to *tell* people that)!" Patrik confided.[114] Harris herself best summed up the synergy: "Blues and barbecue, it's a love thing. I love to give these musicians this barbecue because it's what they love. They love to give me this blues because that's what I love."[115] Harris semiretired when Naber sold Grand Emporium in 2004. That closure did not dampen musicians' and patrons' love of Harris and all that she had done for Kansas City's barbecue reputation.

Earl Quick

Also laying Kansas City's barbecue foundations were Tony Sielman and Anthony Rieke of Rosedale Bar-B-Q (see chapter 10). Sielman's nephew Earl Quick was their protégée. The first Quick's Barbecue sat at 2725 Brown Avenue in Kansas City, Kansas, in what had at one time been Bonnie Bar B.Q., operated by Helen Coble. At this location, Earl, with help of his brother Jim, began perfecting his craft.[116] The restaurant's second iteration, Earl Quick's Bar-B-Q at 1007 Merriam Lane, is better remembered.

From 1964 onward, Earl and his son Ron abided by one principle for smoking meat: only native hickory went into the pit. That wood renders the meat smoky and sweet, distinguishing Kansas City barbecue from mesquite-infused Texas barbecue. Ron, who took over in the mid-1990s, continued his father's habit: "I never did rubs," he explained. The meat should speak for itself after it takes up its hickory undertones.[117]

Specialties that made Quick's stand out from the competition hearkened back to techniques Earl had learned at Rosedale, especially smoking meat but sometimes going one step further and deep-frying it. Ron applied the technique to chicken and the beloved "Bolo" sandwich, or "Oklahoma Tenderloin," for which he smoked ten-pound chubs of baloney and cut them into slices to deep-fry. "He sells an average of 40 to 50 pounds of baloney per month," marveled American Royal Barbeque judge Ardie Davis.[118]

When Quick's celebrated its fiftieth anniversary in 2014, the family decided it was time to close. They kept up the catering, but meat costs had skyrocketed, and construction along Merriam Lane made access to the restaurant difficult. It also made sense to close the restaurant at its pitch point of popularity. Ferruzza labeled it Kansas City, Kansas' "iconic barbecue spot" in his elegiac tribute.[119]

"THE PRIMACY OF AMERICAN CASUAL": JIMMY AND MARY'S, MAJESTIC, GOLDEN OX, COLONY AND LAFFOON'S FRONTIER STEAKHOUSES

Jimmy and Mary's and the Majestic

Betty Fussell did not mean that steakhouses were cheap when she wrote *Raising Steaks: The Life and Times of American Beef*, from which the preceding subtitle is taken. Rather, she was referring to the steakhouse's egalitarian ethos: "We're all equal wearing denim or eating steak," she wrote.[120] From the mid-1950s to the 1980s, even the fancier Kansas City steakhouses refused to put on airs, and many who found a French restaurant intimidating gladly celebrated special occasions at a steakhouse that did not demand formality. That takes us to two early icons: Jimmy and Mary's at 3400 Main Street and the Majestic at Thirty-First and Holmes Streets.

Jimmy and Mary's came of age when jazz pulsed along Main Street and people knew the "American Songbook" by heart. Often open until 4:00 a.m., it was the go-to for hungry performers after their gigs. There, they sat down to sizzling garlic-buttered steaks served alongside that Missouri favorite, spaghetti red, in which spaghetti is mixed with chili. Initially, steak was hard to come by, given war rationing, so Mary Tidona and her business partner, Clella "Jimmy" Goodwin, started their careers with a hamburger stand at Broadway and Armour Boulevards. With their success and World War II coming to an end, Tidona risked moving the location and serving more expensive fare. Goodwin left at that point, and Louis Sholtz became Tidona's business partner and, soon thereafter, her husband. Keeping the name Jimmy and Mary's, the couple moved to Main Street in 1944.[121]

Tidona took charge after she and Sholtz divorced. A cozy atmosphere characterized the restaurant's two-thousand-square-foot space. Regulars crowded in, with Liberace, Peter Falk and Merle Haggard among the host of celebrities who frequented the restaurant when they were in town.[122] From 1950 onward, Jimmy and Mary's shared the building with Davey's Uptown Ramblers Club, also an intimate venue. A swinging door separated the two, with the restaurant relying on Davey's to supply cocktails. Many patrons spent much of their evenings listening to music at Davey's or nearby Milton's Taproom before slipping into Jimmy and Mary's when hunger hit.

After a 1980 fire temporarily shut down the restaurant, Tidona's grandson Frank Macaluso took over, allowing Tidona more time to mingle with guests. But business suffered, as traffic on Main Street declined in the 1980s. By 1994, the steakhouse had closed.[123] Nonetheless, Jimmy and Mary's reminded former patrons of a time when the Tidona family kept night owls well fed as they soaked up Main Street entertainment.

However, back in the 1940s, when midtown nightlife was thriving, Majestic Steakhouse resided less than a mile away from Jimmy and Mary's, at Thirty-First and Holmes Streets. While musicians favored Jimmy and Mary's, the Kansas City Athletics and visiting ball players favored the Majestic, where they mixed with regulars who soaked up proprietor Salvatore "Tudie" Lusco's hospitality. He opened his restaurant in 1944, after being discharged from the army, and by the war's end, the Majestic was eager to give a hungry nation the thick-cut steaks and prime rib dinners it craved.

Lusco filled his steakhouse with baseball memorabilia. Diners gazed at autographed baseballs from major-league teams, along with bats and balls from each World Series. Joe DiMaggio, Mickey Mantle and Ted Williams were among the restaurant's loyal patrons, along with sports journalists. Their devotion was partly the result of Lusco's warmth and generosity. Every spring training "since Kansas City has had a major-league team," wrote Landon Laird, Lusco traveled to West Palm Beach, Florida, to give the Athletics "a big steak dinner."[124]

The Lusco hospitality heritage stretched back to the Pendergast era, when, in 1930, Lusco and his brother Jim started their careers with Club Royale at Independence and Troost Avenue, followed by supper clubs that attracted unemployed musicians to Kansas City because there was money to be made in Lusco's establishments. Reminiscing in 1973, after he had retired and passed the restaurant to his nephew Santo, Lusco explained to a reporter that bootleg liquor kept his own family eating—not just the musicians' families. "It was a wide-open town. Horse racing was over

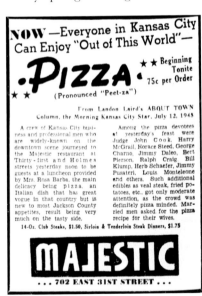

A Majestic advertisement in the *Kansas City Times* (November 26, 1946). *From www.newspapers.com.*

in Riverside; a crap table was at just about every saloon; candy stores and drugstores had slot machines. Sinful? No," Lusco maintained.[125]

Culinarily speaking, Lusco's success with pizza is as significant as his success with steak. Along with Teresa Bondon at the Italian Gardens and Ed Bruni at Gaetano's (see chapter 8), Lusco served pizza at the Majestic and advertised it heavily from 1946 onward. Bread dough, anchovies, tomatoes and cheese awakened jaded appetites but used minimal ration points.

The Majestic suffered the same fate as Jimmy and Mary's when midtown lost its popularity. After Lusco's death in 1978, Santo closed the restaurant.[126] Nonetheless, powerful memories of the Majestic led Doug Barnard to open the New Majestic Steakhouse in what had been Fitzpatrick's Saloon at 931 Broadway Boulevard. Today, it operates as the Majestic Restaurant and Jazz Club and is owned by Jolyn and Frank Sebree III. Thus, the heritage of whiskey, steak and jazz live on in Kansas City.

The Golden Ox

Midtown was removed from the intensely physical reality of the West Bottoms Stockyards, which supplied the Majestic and Jimmy and Mary's with their beef, but after the war's end and with rationing gone, Jay B. Dillingham reasoned that it was time for a serious steakhouse to open in the West Bottoms. As president of the Kansas City Stock Yard Company, Dillingham wanted a place "for the guys out in the yards…to come in and eat and have a good, hot meal, have a steak," explained the last general manager, Mike Holland.[127]

The Golden Ox, which opened in 1949 in the Livestock Exchange Building, was precisely that. The stockyards were still trading around eight million cattle yearly, and their personnel relied on the steakhouse for leisure, as well as business.[128] As such, the restaurant's atmosphere and environment reflected its clientele's pragmatic needs. As late as 2005, when Jane and Michael Stern featured the restaurant in *Roadfood*, even the chairs were still "cleverly designed for gents to rest their cowboy hats just beneath the seat." Ferruzza noted that long after the stockyards closed in 1991, many clients were still wearing cowboy hats.[129] Pretense was nonexistent.

The menu focused on in-house fabricated, dry-aged steak, with few concessions to lighter appetites. Significantly, many credit the Golden Ox with originating the Kansas City strip steak, including Congressman Victor

A postcard depicting the Golden Ox, circa 1950s. *Author's collection.*

L. Anfuso from New York, who told fellow representatives in 1962 that "it was in these stockyards in Kansas City that the now-familiar Kansas City sirloin steak originated," something that "even we New Yorkers prefer." Anfuso was referencing Dillingham's decision to open a Golden Ox Restaurant in Washington, D.C.—for some decades, Washington, D.C.'s only nonlocal steakhouse—located on L Street.[130]

The Golden Ox survived different owners, various tragedies and economic downturns, most significantly, the Flood of 1951, which was followed by stockyard and meatpacking closures. The steakhouse itself suffered a brief shutdown in 2003, before local investors, led by Bill Teel and Steve Greer, bought the Golden Ox.[131] Even though the restaurant underwent a cleaning and added barbecue options, Teel and Greer did not tamper with the grill or décor, keeping both as they had been. It was not enough. As Ferruzza explained on KCUR's *Central Standard*, Kansas Citians liked the fact that the Ox was there, but they did not often go to the restaurant, so it closed.[132]

Much like the Majestic, however, the shuttering of the Golden Ox shook Kansas Citians, especially Chef Wes Gartner and Jill Myers, who had recently opened their West Bottoms restaurant, Voltaire. In 2018, after the Golden Ox had been vacant for four years, the two renovated a portion of the original building and reopened it. While their Golden Ox uses new recipes and is a new restaurant, it focuses on steak and relies on loyal patrons who learned the last time to support the restaurants that matter to them and their city's heritage.[133]

Ralph Gaines Colony Steak House

Jay B. Dillingham, restaurateurs will confide, could be a difficult man to work with. In fact, without his difficult personality, Kansas City might have had fewer steakhouse options—most importantly, it might not have had Ralph Gaines Colony Steak House. Its first location in the Ambassador Hotel at 3560 Broadway Boulevard placed it in the great age of hotel dining, but unlike most hotel restaurants, steak took priority both on the menu and in the restaurant's name, and when it moved to Union Station, it became one of the city's most popular restaurants, steakhouse or otherwise. However, the Gaines family's story is one of a city's hospitality industry in transition.

Ralph Gaines, a restaurant man with an MBA from the University of Chicago, was working in Chicago's legendary Blackhawk Restaurant when Dillingham contacted him. Making Gaines an offer he could not refuse, Gaines and his wife, Betty, moved to Kansas City, and he became Golden Ox's general manager.[134] Quickly, Gaines's talents made him his boss's rival, and as the story goes, Gaines decided to leave Dillingham before he was fired. He secretly opened the Colony while he was still managing the Golden Ox. The Colony's success was immediate, and Dillingham was suspicious. On Christmas Eve in 1953, Dillingham confronted Gaines, asking if he owned the Colony. Gaines responded in the affirmative, so Dillingham ordered him to hand over his Golden Ox keys to Paul Robinson, the new general manager.[135] Robinson himself would take what he had learned about the business and likewise leave Golden Ox to join Joe and Bill Gilbert to create their own steakhouses, most notably the Inn at the Landing and Plaza III.

Gaines's enthusiasm for steak and for his patrons was legendary. He involved himself in everything from choosing, fabricating and dry aging his beef to knowing his customers by name. And on busy nights, he took orders and ran food. The Colony recalls the 1950s, when Kansas City's crossroads reputation was at its apex. Scores of people congregated downtown for entertainment and dining. Perhaps most significantly, Ralph was at his best when he worked in partnership with others, particularly Betty, who booked the live entertainment that made the Colony a top

Marilyn Maye and the Sammy Tucker Trio performing in the lounge at Ralph Gaines Colony Steak House. *Photograph courtesy of Karen Gaines.*

dining-out choice. The restaurant's most famous singer, Marilyn Maye, booked an eleven-year engagement at the Colony; she loved the audiences and the Gaineses that much.[136]

While a well-aged, perfectly cooked steak can speak for itself, Gaines also learned at the Blackhawk the power of greens, most importantly, salads. He embraced Don Roth's Blackhawk tagline: "Tossed three times so as not to bruise the tender leaves."[137] The dressing was also legendary. "Because of the quantities needed, the dressings were mixed in a washing machine—don't ask me how, as it has always baffled me," commented Gaines's daughter, Karen.

After Ralph Gaines's passing in January 1979, Betty and her children, Bob and Karen, moved the Colony from the Ambassador Hotel to Union Station. The family had opened Landmark Restaurant at Union Station in 1971, but by the mid-1970s, downtown hotel dining was waning, and they wanted to consolidate their operations. For a time, both the Colony and the Gaineses' other Union Station restaurant, the Lobster Pot, continued to thrive, although Union Station was literally deteriorating. In 1989, Union

Station officially closed, and the Gaines family entered what Ferruzza described as a "nomadic period," until 1994, when they opened their final restaurant, the Colony Steakhouse & Lobster Pot at Eighty-Eighth Street and State Line Road. By 2002, the restaurant had seen a 20 percent decline in sales because of the weak economy, and Bob Gaines was ready to leave the business to practice law full time. The metro area had expanded beyond that part of the State Line Road corridor, and by 2003, when the restaurant was closed, many independent steakhouses had been struggling against an invasion of corporate chains at all price points, from Ryan's to Morton's.

However, for multiple generations, Ralph Gaines Colony Steak House was special, recalling the glamor of downtown dining with live entertainment and highballs, the glamor of arriving to Kansas City by train, the wonder of stepping up to a lavish salad bar and the comfort of knowing the Gaines family on a first-name basis, not to mention Ralph's care and regard for the food he sold.

Laffoon's Frontier Steakhouse

Another standout for its distinctiveness was Laffoon's Frontier Steakhouse at Ninety-Fourth Street and State Avenue in Kansas City, Kansas. For its sixty-year existence, the same family owned and ran it. It was founded in 1960 by Everette "Dutch" and Mary Laffoon. The couple started with a four-table café, a Phillips 66, some guest cabins and a family home on a stretch of State Avenue in the country. When the couple tore down the gas station and created Frontier Steakhouse, Mary oversaw the kitchen and worked at the restaurant until she retired in 2010 at the age of ninety. The Laffoons' sons, Dennis and Ron, ran the restaurant when their father passed away. Locals were as steady in their custom as the owners were in their service.

This was a place that supported youth sports and where the Kiwanis Club met, where couples held rehearsal dinners and where, on Wednesday nights, regulars listened to the Hole in the Wall Gang perform their music and watched Dennis "step away from serving fried chicken and pork chops to do one heck of an Elton John impersonation," Ted B. Meadows recalled fondly. The service was fantastic, with a waitstaff "there to take your order and deliver your food, not to convince you that they would rather be somewhere else," Meadows added.[138]

The menu was as unpretentious as the service. It offered four char-broiled steaks: a T-bone, a filet, a Kansas City strip or ground sirloin, plus a daily steak special. The meals came with mushroom gravy, a potato, a salad, a vegetable and a fresh-baked roll. Weekends were popular for prime rib dinners. People appreciated the fact that Frontier never instituted à la carte service and remained affordable. Its distinctiveness, as Meadows observed, was that it was not some "theme restaurant" or "curated experience"; rather, it was "simple and unpretentious and come-as-you-are."

As was the case with many restaurants, COVID-19 spelled financial disaster for the Laffoon's Frontier Steakhouse. The family sorrowfully closed the restaurant in December 2020. The pandemic was not the only reason the restaurant closed; taxes and a building in need of repairs contributed to the decision. The Frontier had witnessed its address transition from a country road to a metropolis, a mile from the Kansas Speedway and shopping complexes. It weathered food fads and trends, withstood corporatization, remained within one family and resisted slick advertising. Its closure saddened the community, and it makes Ron Laffoon's words seem like a kind of portent: "From the bottom of our heart, please support your local businesses."[139]

Kansas City-Style Upscale Dining

With its economy historically associated with agribusiness, Kansas City did not have a strong fine-dining heritage. Restaurant critic Jess Ritter pointed out in 1976, "We do not have any restaurants known for decades or generations of high excellence like those that can be found in Chicago, New York, London and Paris."[140] Those that did rise to prominence were not mere imitations of fancy East Coast or European restaurants, however. They appealed to Kansas Citians' values and played a fundamental role in building the city's own culinary heritage by establishing traditions that are still in place today (albeit not with the need for dress codes and table captains). Chapter 2 covers fine dining associated with hotels and transportation; this chapter covers stand-alone restaurants and their evolution from the 1940s through the 2000s.

POSTWAR GLAMOUR: BRETTON'S RESTAURANT, PUTSCH'S 210 AND EDDYS' RESTAURANT

Bretton's

Bretton's challenged the belief that Kansas City's fine dining was restricted to oysters, lobster and steak. Owner and former Rabbi Max Bretton downplayed those mainstays in favor of continental cuisine that took diners from Russia to Vienna. Over its thirty years in business, the restaurant was so beloved that a *Squire* 2005 readers' poll ranked it Kansas City's number one restaurant of the twentieth century—in part because Max Bretton understood that in the right setting, food was a salve that healed the spirit and imparted good will.[141]

Max and Mary Bretton moved to Kansas City in 1931, when Max became the director of the Jewish Community Center and, shortly afterward, the Jewish Welfare Federation; however, he thought running a restaurant might offer him more opportunities to put his convictions into action. As he explained to Mary, "A restaurant is nothing more than a community center with food." They knew how to entertain, and after all, as Max pointed out, he knew how to run a community center. We might "do it in a larger home."[142]

Convinced, the Brettons purchased Weiss Café at 1215 Baltimore in 1945–46 (see chapter 9). Across from the Orpheum Theater and close to the Music Hall, Bretton's became popular with the "literati, artists, and visiting notables," wrote WHB's *Swing* in 1947. Waiter Ray Starzmann marveled at how many celebrities he waited on: "Isaac Stern, Roberta Peters, Victor Borge. They would walk over from the Music Hall…to eat spaghetti Caruso or peaches Melba," he told Charles Ferruzza. Max's daughter, Deborah Bretton Granoff, agreed: "Many performers made Bretton's their dining headquarters when in Kansas City for engagements."[143]

At Bretton's, many Kansas Citians first tasted chicken paprika and coq au vin. The restaurant's chicken Kiev was particularly well regarded. Mary Schwieger, the wife of the Kansas City Philharmonic conductor Hans Schwieger, sent Max a postcard from Russia telling him that, while touring, she and Hans ordered chicken Kiev in every city "but have never found any that equals Bretton's."[144] The restaurant's chefs were acclaimed. Augustine "Gus" Riedi who would later go on to open the acclaimed French restaurant La Bonne Auberge, produced Escoffier classics like sole meuniere. Josef Berkowitz, from Poland, excelled in Ashkenazi Jewish cuisine. His roast capon and rich chicken broth with giant matzo balls were especially popular.

In 1954, Bretton added the Bali Hai Room, Kansas City's prominent tiki bar and Polynesian restaurant. This idea, recounted Granoff, came from her parents' love of Don the Beachcomber in Chicago. The bar's potent cocktails had people flooding through its doors. Charles Broomfield remembered the Atomic Bomb: "You were restricted to two," he recounted, "and the challenge was to see if you could get up the stairs without help!"[145] Its Polynesian food "was equally outstanding," said Granoff. Chinese chefs ensured that new hires were trained to produce the same dishes with the same consistency. Granoff's favorite was mandarin duck, pressed and crisped in peanut oil and served with plum sauce.

Bretton's also assumed a courageous role in challenging segregation. Fellowship House, an interracial organization, sought Max's agreement to allow members a table for its Wednesday luncheons. Max agreed "in hopes that the Restaurant Owners Association would find the courage to jettison Jim Crow," wrote historian Sherry Lamb Schirmer.[146] The thinking was that patrons would witness interracial socializing for what it was—normal. One patron, indignant that Black people were dining in the restaurant, told Max that he would not return. "My father put his arm around him, looked him in the eye, and gently said, 'I will miss you,'" recalled Granoff. That humanitarian spirit lay within Bretton's heart. Shortly after Bretton's passing, Reverend Rodney Crewse of St. James Catholic Church wrote, "Dear Max was blind to your color, blind to your religion, blind to your sex or age— Max was so blind that he made everybody see a little better."[147] Bretton's Restaurant set a gold standard in hospitality that matched its cuisine.

Putsch's 210

Bretton's epitomized downtown fine dining, while Putsch's 210 epitomized fine dining on the Plaza. Its service, lighting, soft live music and tableside cooking were carried out with graceful exactitude. Virginia and Jud Putsch opened their restaurant in 1947, after purchasing Clair Martin's Cafeteria and Plaza Tavern in the Triangle Building. The Putsches kept the cafeteria concept while transforming the 210 West Forty-Seventh Street address into a restaurant that Martin would not recognize, "from the white kitchen to the main dining room in deep emerald, with a starlight ceiling and grill work in the wall outline suggestive of New Orleans." A "mural on the bar mirror also has a Southern touch," wrote a reporter. It reflected Virginia's North Carolina upbringing, her "starting point in the design motif."[148] The menu also reflected Virginia's love of New Orleans–style dishes, noted Mary Sanchez, the daughter of Chef de Cuisine Herman Sanchez.[149]

Diners began their nights with cocktails mixed by Willie Grandison, who would later finish his career at the American Restaurant. Appetizers such as escargots chablisienne followed. Table captains prepared the 210 Special Salad of Kentucky Limestone lettuce, anchovies, a chopped egg and Danish bleu cheese before diners moved on to their mains, such as tableside-flambéed steak Diane, Shrimp Creole or red snapper throats. Charles Ballew

Gourmet Dinner for Two
*
Green Turtle Consomme, au Sherry
*
Baked Crabmeat Savannah, in Coquille
*
Raspberry Ice
*
Cornish Game Hen on Flaming Sword
*
Wild Rice   Fresh Brussels Sprouts with Green Grapes
*
Hot French Bread
*
Kentucky Limestone Lettuce with Lemon Oil Dressing
*
Flaming Bananas Foster
*
Coffee

Chateau Olivier (Half Bottle)   **$30.00**
Taylor Champagne (Half Bottle)

Top: A postcard depicting Putsch's 210, circa the early 1950s. *Author's collection.*

Bottom: "Gourmet Dinner for Two," Putsch's 210 menu (1971). *Author's collection.*

remembered "all the famous flaming desserts: crêpes Suzette, cherries jubilee, bananas Foster."[150]

Chef Sanchez, who was an infant when his mother came to the United States from Mexico City, grew up in Armourdale, Kansas City, Kansas, and started his career washing dishes at the Muehlebach Hotel before working through the stations of Escoffier's brigade de cuisine. At Putsch's 210, he put in "ten, twelve, sometimes fourteen hours a day," recalled Mary Sanchez, who remembered her mother starching her father's chef's hats and tucking the metal squares into his back brace—necessary for a hefty man who stood on concrete floors, stirring, chopping, sautéing."[151]

The restaurant withstood industry pressures to resort to processed foods instead relying on its chefs. Rather, the threat to Putsch's 210 was simply the natural progression of its restaurateurs' lives and its new owner, Montgomery Ward, who had neither roots in Kansas City nor experience in the fine-dining sector. Although the restaurant closed in 1973, Putsch's 210, with its dress code, strolling violinist and tableside cooking, signified for Kansas Citians the passing of an era that they would reminisce about for the rest of their lives.

Eddys' Restaurant

By the late 1940s, Kansas City was awash with supper clubs, where entertainment accompanied food that was served late into the night. With so many supper clubs in the city, why have another? Skeptics asked that question when Eddys' was under construction. "We'll give them a month to stay open," laughed the wiseacres. The Eddy brothers, Landon Laird maintained, had the last laugh.[152]

The brothers' success stemmed, in part, from their care in what their guests ate, which was unusual for a club, where entertainment usually took precedence. George, Ned and Sam Eddy maintained "that good food contributed half the enjoyment to a good show....You could get a three-pound lobster or a ham sandwich, and each would be delectable," maintained Laird.[153] That commitment to food showed up in Eddys' opening announcement in February 1949. More than $100,000 was invested in the kitchen alone, ensuring each department had its own refrigeration. "Even the garbage was refrigerated," Jim Eddy, Ned's son, remembered.[154]

The family had "restauranting in their veins," wrote Laird. The brothers initially opened Plaza Bowl at 430 Alameda Road, combining bowling with

Eddys' menu, undated. *Courtesy of Jim Eddy.*

a coffee shop and cocktail lounge. After World War II, the brothers subleased J.C. Nichols's downtown parking lot at the corner of Thirteenth Street and Baltimore Avenue, under which they built Eddys'.[155] The restaurant's dining room included a lower-level dance floor that was surrounded on three sides by a raised area for tables and booths with décor copied from George Eddy's Cadillac. "Outside of some car manufacturers and the Pullman Company," George told a reporter, "no one else had that English whipcord covering."[156] Similar to Putsch's 210, the dining room sported New Orleans–style pillars with hand-wrought ironwork.

For many, the restaurant's best meal was late-night supper with lush chafing-dish specials, including shrimp curry and sautéed lobster. Such dishes brought in performers who were coming off shows elsewhere and patrons who were hungry after a night of dancing. "Tony DiPardo, showman of the trumpet," led the house band in the restaurant's first decade, recalled Jim Eddy. George Eddy handled bookings, bringing in performers for two-week gigs working the New York–Vegas circuit. Andy Williams, Nelson Eddy, the Crew Cuts, Eydie Gormé and countless others performed American Songbook classics. Kansas City's downtown area felt "like a little New York

City," recalled Jim Eddy, and Eddys' was in the center of the action, until the rise of television, that is.

A three-minute act on *Dick Clark* or *Ed Sullivan* netted performers the same—or more—money than they made working the circuit. Supper clubs began closing, "and meanwhile, downtown Kansas City was starting to take a forty-year nap," Jim Eddy ruefully added. By 1964, Eddys' had done away with most of its live entertainment and focused on food, dropping prices by 30 percent. It was not enough, so the Eddy family plotted new ventures, including Eddys' Loaf 'n Stein, the George Eddy family's Chateau le Boeuf at the Prom Sheraton on Sixth and Main Streets and Eddys' South at 103rd Street and State Line Road. But when Kansas Citians of a certain age crave the old-fashioned supper club atmosphere, at the top of their wish list is a reincarnation of Eddys', the best of its class.

SUNSET OF AN ERA: LA MEDITERRANEE AND AMERICAN RESTAURANT

On the surface, La Mediterranee and the American Restaurant had little in common, aside from their exclusivity and high prices. One specialized in the painstaking haute French cooking associated with Carême and Escoffier, while the other consciously rejected French food to highlight the bounty of the United States and its own culinary traditions. However, their ascents and declines illustrate the tension that Kansas City's poshest restaurants experienced when it came to attracting loyal patrons while trying to maintain a national reputation. They also survived long enough to show a transition away from fine dining as it had been understood for centuries (an à la carte menu, tableside cooking and a dress code) toward contemporary casual restaurants that largely came to replace them.

La Mediterranee

La Mediterranee opened in 1971, becoming "indisputably Kansas City's premier French restaurant," wrote *Kansas City Star* restaurant critic John Martellaro. A couple "could sneak away for a romantic dinner or treat a Madison Avenue lawyer to dinner without apologizing for Midwestern fare and service," added C.C. Hallquist of the *Town Squire*.[157] The building at 4742 Pennsylvania had earlier housed the Oyster Bay, and when Toussaint

The entrance to La Mediterranee. *Photograph by Dory DeAngelo (1991), courtesy of Missouri Valley Special Collections, Kansas City Public Library (Kansas City, MO).*

and Lise Moallic leased the space, Lise appreciated the décor. "It is absolutely, really the sea," she decided, and despite Toussaint's hesitations that people could not pronounce it, La Mediterranee became the restaurant's name.[158]

Characterized as "small and intimate," La Mediterranee quickly became popular due to its delicious food, all prepared from scratch. "You in America have the béarnaise, the hollandaise, the mayonnaise, all in cans. We have no cans," Lise told Jane P. Fowler.[159] Toussaint, with the help of Sous Chef J.M. Gerbout, prepared the sauces on which French cuisine is based; they also fabricated veal, deboned quail and scaled fish.

When the Moallics decided to return to California, another husband-and-wife team, Gilbert and Hannelore Jahnier, took over in 1977. They kept the name and arguably enhanced the restaurant's reputation for haute cuisine, expanding and remodeling it. The *Clarendon Guide to Kansas City Restaurants* ranked only it and Jasper's as Kansas City's two top restaurants. Its "quiet elegance," French waiters, a bouillabaisse requiring two weeks' notice and the wine list were highly praised.[160]

Because of its high price tag and cuisine that was unusual to many Kansas Citians, La Mediterranee was for the most special occasions. Lyric Opera baritone Brian Steele, for instance, remembered celebrating his twentieth

La Mediterranee's menu from the *Kansas City Star* (February 20, 1972). *From www.newspapers.com.*

anniversary there, relishing the opportunity to "dress up and go first-class: candlelight, crystal, and champagne." It was an evening of "pampered excellence."[161] Many started their dinners with classic French preparations, such as foie gras du Périgord, presented as twin circles studded with shaved black truffle, along with cornichon and red onion garnish and tiny cubes of amber Sauternes wine jelly.

Regardless, the trend toward casual dining was accelerating. Across the street from La Mediterranee was Gilbert-Robinson's wildly popular Houlihan's Old Place, a bellwether in the ever-competitive restaurant industry. *French* increasingly meant unapproachable and intimidating, with dining protocols that embarrassed the uninitiated customer. In 1993, J.C. Nichols Company refused to renew La Mediterranee's lease and instead offered the Jahniers the smaller 602 West Forty-Eight Street address, where the House of Toy Chinese restaurant resided (see chapter 9). Jahnier bluntly told the *Kansas City Star* that Nichols "had treated them like dirt."[162]

For ten months, La Mediterranee had no home; then the owners moved to Overland Park, Kansas. They took their chandeliers, oil paintings, marble fireplace and mantel to the new location to remind patrons of their old home. The space was large and "visually appealing," wrote Martellaro in March 1994, with "beautifully appointed dining rooms," but the restaurant was becoming a relic. "People don't like to dress up like they used to," Jahnier admitted, "so we don't enforce a tie and jacket like we used to."[163] The Jahniers loosened the atmosphere even further, streamlining the menu and offering early bird specials. It was of no avail. La Mesa Mexican restaurant took over the address in 1999.

Significantly, Jahnier's 1990s creations were strikingly contemporary and inspiring to a generation of up-and-coming chefs, especially delights like the potato pancakes that sandwiched seared foie gras, tart Granny Smith apples and shaved black truffle. "I can still taste it in my mind," wrote Martellaro, who named it one of his top-ten dishes of 1994.[164] The food was fresh and creative—what should remain in our minds, even if dress codes, thick drapery and a requisite number of courses for dinner ultimately defeated La Mediterranee.

The American Restaurant

When the American Restaurant opened in 1974, it maintained exclusive trappings of fine dining but promoted American cuisine as being worthy of just as much respect as French cuisine. Yet this jewel in Hallmark's Crown Center faced many of La Mediterranee's same challenges when it came to finding loyal patrons who would support its culinary ambitions.

Don and Adele Hall brought in James Beard and Barbara Kafka to help devise the menu, while Joe Baum and architect Warren Platner created a spectacular space in which the meals would unfold. Diners entered the restaurant on top of the Crown Center via a bar and lounge before descending a grand staircase to the dining room, where floor-to-ceiling louvered windows looked out over the skyline. As his Valentine to the Hall family, Platner fashioned oak columns that "branched into a canopy of elongated hearts," while "lacy rosette-topped pillars" gave the room a Modernist "dining under the trees" feel, wrote Pete Dulin.[165] Diners perused an equally modern menu. No more "pseudo-French, pseudo-German, pseudo-Italian," general manager Gerard F. Brach promised.[166]

Four chefs best illustrate the American's importance to Kansas City's culinary history: Bradley Ogden, Rex Hale, Debbie Gold and Michael Smith. Ogden took the helm in 1979 and was critical to fulfilling Brach's promise. He featured his Midwestern interpretation of Joe Baum's New York Four Seasons Restaurant, keeping the restaurant's focus on American regional specialties, such as Missouri cured ham and Maryland soft-shelled crabs, but treating them with sophisticated culinary techniques. Dishes seldom associated with fine dining, such as "Grandma's wild greens" or a chicken breast with Applejack and chestnut dressing, also made diners reconsider their prejudices toward treating humble foods as strictly humble. Under Ogden's reign, the American received significant recognition.

His departure in 1983 put the city's most expensive restaurant on unstable footing, however. The restaurant's price tag had done little to gain regular patrons, and Kansas City only had so many visitors to rely on to break even. When Rex Hale took over in 1989, he was tasked with regaining the fourth

Crown Center with the mayor's Christmas tree. American Restaurant can be seen in the background (circa 2015). *Courtesy of Missouri Valley Special Collections, Kansas City Public Library (Kansas City, MO).*

Mobil star the restaurant had lost in 1988, and he had the clout to do so. Hale already understood the American's mission, having worked there previously as sous chef. He returned after working as the executive chef at Dallas's famed Baby Routh restaurant and set to work revamping the American's menu while the restaurant closed for renovation.

When it reopened in 1990, Hale not only recouped the fourth Mobile star but attracted "ambassadors, movie stars, statesmen, and tycoons," wrote *Ingram's*.[167] He introduced Kansas City diners to New American cuisine, a style that celebrated American immigrants' culinary contributions, along with regional foodstuffs. Hale's virtuosity left diners swooning when they sat down to dishes such as potato-crusted snapper with braised wild mushrooms and red pepper vinaigrette. The American is now "a crucible for New American cuisine," declared *Esquire* restaurant critic John Mariani.[168]

The Crown Center's gamble on Hale had paid off—but at what cost? Martellaro called it a "monumental blunder," given the 1990s' recession. Management had "deliberately priced itself out of the reach of 90 percent of the city's populace," when, despite its accolades, the profit margin stayed flat. Patrons walked in unaware of the formality and price and then walked right back out.[169] Hale was replaced by Jim Ackard as management abruptly changed course.

The American always strove to meet multiple, often conflicting, expectations. Approachable food, what most Kansas Citians preferred, did not work well with the price point that the restaurant wished to maintain; after all, explicit "casualization" (industry speak for lower prices) would defeat the restaurant's reputation as Kansas City's premier restaurant. The confusion surrounding the American's purpose at its management level resulted in many chefs' short tenures at the restaurant, but the American was still approaching iconic status.

This was likely due to Michael Smith and Debbie Gold, who shared the executive chef position from 1994 to 2001. They raised the restaurant's profile to its highest level and initiated the popular James Beard dinners. Visiting chefs prepared meals, and equally as important, Smith noted, they mentored the American's young line cooks, many of whom remained in Kansas City to work in and/or open their own restaurants.[170]

Gold and Smith embraced a Midwestern culinary sensibility without a "premeditated style," other than "simple elegance."[171] The prosciutto and Crenshaw melon terrine with a port wine glaze and the Napoleon of crisp-fried potato sheets, layered with artichokes, peas and roasted tomatoes, were standouts, and in the couple's first four years at the restaurant, its revenues went up 28 percent. Some came for the restaurant's playful takes on school lunch dishes, like mushroom-stuffed rigatoni with Montasio cheese, others came for squash stuffed with peekytoe crab.

Gold and Smith received the 1999 James Beard Best Chefs Midwest Award; this was the same year that the American celebrated its twenty-fifth anniversary. But Smith recalled the event as a "kick in the gut." When he left the New York City ceremony to call the restaurant and report the news, "there were no diners in the restaurant," he later told Jill Wendholt Silva. Smith "started to realize the American was fairly irrelevant."[172] He also recalled a night when the dining room was empty except for a table of four men, who removed their suit jackets after being seated. When their food was ready, they were told they must put their jackets back on, but instead of agreeing, they left. Smith and Gold were perturbed by the dress code and how it actively worked against the restaurant's ability to attract patrons.[173] They departed to open Forty Sardines in Leawood, Johnson County, Kansas.

The American's final chef, Michael Corvino, took the grandest culinary stage in Kansas City when the restaurant celebrated its fortieth anniversary in 2014, but behind the scenes, the restaurant was financially gasping. The dress code had finally been eliminated, and the bar offered patrons a cheaper alternative to the grand dining room below—but with no success. The restaurant was closed in 2016 and transformed into an event pop-up space.

In some ways, La Mediterranee could not escape a cumbersome, off-putting name. Similarly, the American could not escape its most striking feature: the Platner-designed dining room, which could not generate a more relaxed vibe, speculated Silva. But as with many American chefs before him, Corvino stayed in Kansas City to open Corvino's Supper Club. As the following section details, Kansas City became home to an eclectic array of chef-driven restaurants, inspired by the boundaries that La Mediterranee and the American pushed.

Breaking Away: Fedora Café & Bar and Café Allegro

Two other 1970s restaurants, the Prospect and Harry Starker's, were already taking advantage of loosening dining etiquette to create imaginative but approachable spaces for patrons to enjoy gourmet food and ambiance. The next significant breakthroughs came in the 1980s, with Gilbert-Robinson's Café Fedora and Steve Cole's Café Allegro. Both eschewed rigidities, creating a zeitgeist whose vestiges remain with us.

Fedora Café & Bar

Back in the day, reminisced Charles Ferruzza, Fedora "was as sexy and vibrant as Nicole Kidman in *Moulin Rouge*."[174] That characterization resonated with those who made the "Hat," as it was nicknamed, their destination. The restaurant did precisely what Paul Robinson of Gilbert-Robinson (G-R) wished—it attracted patrons who had "evolved from the '70s singles scene catered to by Houlihan's," their other wildly popular but more casual Plaza restaurant.[175]

Fedora opened in 1983 at 210 West Forty-Seventh Street, where Putsch's 210 had once resided. But G-R reached back further than Putsch's 210 for inspiration, back to the vogue for fedora hats and Clair Martin's 1930s Plaza Tavern, where live jazz pulsed and bright young things drank cocktails and slurped oysters.

A smart but understated décor of tile floors, rose-colored walls and gray flannel upholstery helped Fedora's patrons focus on the food. Chefs controlled the kitchen and menu with "open cooking stations in the middle of the dining room that allowed for visual and aromatic sensations," wrote Chef Jesse John Vega Jr. of his time there. "The charcuterie station dished out liver pâtés and wafer-thin slices of beef tartare, served on a chilled plate smeared with parmesan aioli," he remembered.[176] Chefs created

A Café Fedora "Fresh Sheet" and Millionaire's Menu. *Courtesy of Jesse John Vega Sr.*

CAVIAR

Featuring Osetra, Sevruga and Exquisite American Caviars Throughout May.

Caviar . . . Black gold. Come indulge yourself with the world's most treasured delicacy in the elegant dining ambiance of Fedora. Share our excitement throughout May as we celebrate a special shipment of fresh American and imported Russian caviar.

Our product is specially purchased from California Sunshine Fine Foods—a Swedish family-owned business largely responsible for the reflourishing American caviar supply. Discover the distinctive tastes of our sevruga-style American Sturgeon roe from Oregon and the apricot pearls of American Golden Whitefish caviar . . . along with genuine Sevruga and Osetra from the Caspian Sea.

Enjoy the luxurious food au naturel with a sparkling wine or chilled Russian vodka, or try one of our special dishes accented with the delicate pearls.

BAR TASTINGS

Every Evening 5-7 PM

We're celebrating the arrival of our fresh caviar with samplings for you to taste at affordable prices. Do something different for the cocktail hour this week . . . visit Fedora and experience the wonderful essence of these caviars.

Imported Osetra . . . . from 6.50
Imported Sevruga . . . from 5.95
American Sturgeon . . from 4.25
American Golden
  Whitefish . . . . . from 2.95

"Fresh Sheets" (daily specials) that incorporated premium perishable ingredients, state-of-the-art cooking and chefs' imaginations. The mesquite grill put a gorgeous char on scallops, halibut, beef tenderloin and lamb chops, while, at the pasta station, the sauté cook tossed house-made pasta. G-R employees traveled across the United States and to Mexico and Europe for inspiration to keep Fedora's menu interesting.[177] Committed to introducing Kansas Citians to new flavors, chefs also made the experience fun for diners. Each evening in May 1985, for example, Fedora featured Russian and American caviars alongside Russian vodkas and sparkling wines.

Jazz and happy hour were likewise a draw. "It felt like a jazz club *should*," David Davis remembered, with a "good-sized stage occupying the east wall and a beautiful, ornate bar on the west wall." While patrons sipped Kir Royale and Cognac, they listened to Angela Hagenbach, Monique Danielle and Tommy Ruskin, among others.[178] Barkeep Harry Murphy held court, offering intelligent conversation and panache.

Fedora reached its apex in the late 1980s. Once it was purchased by Nabil Haddad's Restaurant Group, it became rudderless, with the menu a hodgepodge rather than fashionably eclectic.[179] What had been G-R's most upscale concept quietly became the George Brett Grill in 2003, an event that many today remember with sadness. Nonetheless, during its first decade, Fedora ushered in vibrancy and freedom from stale dictates. It gave talented chefs the license to ignite an ongoing culinary revolution in fine dining.

A Fedora Café promotion from the *Kansas City Star* (May 1985). *From www.newspapers.com.*

Café Allegro

Meanwhile, Steve Cole was blazing his own trail through the culinary landscape. Arguably the first in Kansas City to embrace farm-to-table cuisine and the first in the fine-dining arena to raise awareness of local food insecurity, Cole also made Café Allegro inviting to many people who avoided higher-end restaurants out of social anxiety as much as fear of the cost.

In 1983, the Volker neighborhood was served by a stretch of Thirty-Ninth Street that resembled a small town's Main Street with its own character, but it was conveniently close to Westport and the Plaza. Cole toured Europe to explore restaurant models that might work in Kansas City, keeping in mind those Kansas Citians who had likewise traveled the continent.[180] He transformed a former pizza parlor at 1815 West Thirty-Ninth Street into Café Allegro in 1984, replete with two unusual pieces of equipment for that time in Kansas City: a wood-burning oven and a Cruvinet wine-preserving system that allowed him to serve expensive wines by the glass. It was "a tremendous amount of money for something that was very experimental and hadn't been in the area before," Cole explained, but it and the wood-burning oven paid off.[181]

Diners who could not afford full bottles of wine could then expand their wine knowledge, while wine connoisseurs could sample wines that were unavailable elsewhere in the area. Meanwhile, the wood-burning oven created ambiance and warmth while facilitating Cole's desire to prepare the fresh produce and proteins on his menu, including an impressive array of, as Timothy Finn put it, "criminally fresh" fish. Grilled salmon with Chinese mustard glaze, garnished with Japanese pickled ginger, was a standout. Beef fared equally as well; the filet mignon was oiled, peppered, grilled whole, sliced and served over Maytag blue cheese–enhanced beurre blanc.[182]

Restaurant critics referred to Café Allegro's fare as "cross-cultural," with local ingredients starring in Asian-, Italian- and Californian-influenced dishes. One of Cole's most inspired appetizers was also his simplest, but it demonstrated his confidence in the quality of his raw product: tartare of yellowfin tuna. Cut into tiny cubes and dressed with fried capers, the fish was accented with ginger, scallions, cilantro and sesame oil. Served with sesame crackers and a side of marinated cucumber, it was a revelation in a pre-sashimi-crazed Kansas City.

Cole also helped build a regional food system that contributed to the public's growing love of community-supported agriculture and farmer's markets. The key was Cole's partnership with Mark Marino, the "maestro of tomatoes and the poet of herbs." Marino wanted to build a local gourmet produce market, while Cole wished to buy from one. Marino credited his big break to Café Allegro, explaining that Cole "wouldn't take any junk."[183]

What Cole achieved with local produce was as noteworthy as his creativity with proteins. An eggplant sandwich with grilled prawns or a salad of lamb's quarters, crow's foot and curly dock raised to gourmet status foods that are often brushed off as "hippie fare." And Café Allegro became an icon, anchoring Thirty-Ninth Street's "Restaurant Row" as other chefs began opening a range of eateries there, including Ted Habiger's Room 39 and Scott and Jane Changs' Blue Koi.

Café Allegro could not be forced into a preexisting restaurant category. With sophisticated food, linen tablecloths and wine service, one would assume it demanded money and knowledge of dining etiquette, accompanied by the requisite sneering waiter if one inadvertently committed a faux pax. But no. Repeatedly, Café Allegro was comfortable and friendly. It also avoided the trap that many short-lived upscale restaurants fell into: "artistically arranged plates" lacking substance. Equally important, it did not discourage diners from making a meal of appetizers as a way to save cost but also experience new dishes. Cole's clientele ranged from the casual to dressy, each sitting comfortably alongside the other.

Cole also educated culinary professionals about food insecurity and their obligation to help mitigate it. In 1988, he helped build KC Harvest, an arm of Harvesters Community Food Network, which worked with restaurants to collect and distribute prepared food. He also worked with KC Harvest director Chris Martin to organize a fundraiser in which restaurants put on a buffet at the Savoy Grill to raise money. He organized Kansas City's annual Taste of the Nation and Forks and Corks anti-hunger benefits.[184] Along with Ollie Gates, Cole became as well-known for his philanthropy as he was for his restaurant.

Cole closed Café Allegro at its zenith. In 2002, when the restaurant was ranked number one in Kansas City's *Zagat* survey, he sold it to Hanrahan Investments. He had run Café Allegro for eighteen years and told media sources that he needed "a little bit of a sabbatical." The chefs who trained under and/or followed Cole repeatedly evoke his name, innovations and quest for perfection. The restaurant thus lives on in more than just memory.

6
Cafeterias, Lunch Counters and Casual Good Eats

ood food, well-seasoned," said journalist Rick Bragg of his mother's Appalachian cooking in *Best Cook in the World: Tales from My Momma's Table* (2018). He also characterized the fare dished up at Kansas City's casual eateries in the early to mid-twentieth century. People depended on these places to sustain themselves, and they offered a home away from home. Of course, numerous formal restaurants did that as well, but what made these businesses distinct was their lack of specialization in any one cuisine, their longevity and their celebration of unpretentiousness. Alcohol might have been offered, but the clientele was there to eat more so than to drink. Because the restaurants in this chapter were modest and unassuming, it makes sense that some of them also became ground zero in Kansas City's fight for racial equality: the right to sit and be served, regardless of skin color.

Let's begin with the cafeterias, a concept that originated at the 1893 World's Columbian Exposition in Chicago, and from there, let's relive the days of our iconic lunchrooms, drugstores and neighborhood restaurants, whose names are still recalled by many Kansas Citians.

PLEASE TAKE A TRAY: MYRON GREEN, FORUM AND PUTSCH'S CAFETERIAS

Myron Green

Kansas City's first cafeteria of significance was Myron Green, created by a Michigan dentist-turned-toothpaste-salesman-turned-restaurateur. Green's interest in catering arose from his despair over the subpar meals he ate away from home, especially a meal he ate at a Kohlsaat chain restaurant in Chicago that was presided over by a "big, hard-boiled man cook" who served stale coffee and greasy meat in a steam-filled room. Recognizing that "practically all reasonably priced Chicago restaurants were run on the same plan," Green imagined a cafeteria with food served by expert women cooks. Green ultimately chose to settle in Kansas City, and in 1909, he opened Home Room Lunch Club at 1013 Grand Boulevard. Two German women cooked delicious food, with nothing costing more than five cents. Shortly thereafter, Green opened a second cafeteria, the Colonial, at 1025–27 Main Street, and in 1916, the cafeteria that bore his name, Myron Green, opened at 1113–15 Walnut Street.[185] For around seventy years, Myron Green Cafeterias operated throughout the metro area. Green's ability to set catering trends rather than follow them led to him gaining many competitors.

By leveraging economies of scale, Green offered perennial favorites, like roast or fried chicken, pot pies and corned beef hash. The company's advertising, often reading like newspaper columns, brought in diners who were curious to see if Myron Green stood up to its promises of delicious food that was cheaper than food prepared at home. Historian Samantha Barbas credited the National Restaurant Association, which Green helped found, with presenting women's work outside of the home not as an onus but as a godsend

Can you afford not to do it?

The day of wondering "Can I afford to dine at Myron Green's?" is a thing of the past. Now the question is "How can I afford *not* to dine at Myron Green's?"

Is this new to you? It may be. But it need not be news long, for a simple comparsion will prove to you that Myron Green's delicious woman-cooked food will cost you no more than you've been paying for other kinds. And, when you can get the best. why be satisfied with anything less?

Here are a few examples of what we mean: these are not special prices   they're in effect every day these items are served. These are from to-morrow's menu

Chicken ala King **45**
Myron Green Spaghetti...**35**
Myron Green Swiss Steak .**50**
French Fried Whiting...**30**
Spanish Rice **12**
Large Cinnamon Roll.. .**07**
Delicious Pumpkin Pie.....**15**
Apple Cobbler, a favorite...**10**

A Myron Green advertisement from the *Kansas City Star* (January 30, 1950). *From www.newspapers.com.*

for families who could then enjoy the peace, comfort and expertly prepared food of cafeterias instead of domestic chaos.[186]

Particularly well regarded were Myron Green's baked goods. The Walnut Street location operated a bakery with a lavish window display. Many people stopped in to buy doughnuts and cinnamon rolls for the next day's breakfast before commuting home. They were "home-baked" and "baked by women cooks," as assured by the advertisements.

Inevitably, new dining trends caught up with Myron Green. The company diversified, adding a vending division and concentrating cafeterias in hospitals and office complexes. By the mid-1970s, the name had officially changed to Myron Green Food & Vending. A steep decline of foot traffic downtown caused the company to shutter its original 1115 Walnut Street location, and a long-standing commercial Myron Green Cafeteria, in Mission, Kansas, closed in 1983.

Forum Cafeteria

Many assume that the Forum was named after Rome's public meeting places, but the story relayed by Clarence M. Hayman's biographer was not quite as grand: "Hayman knew no Roman history. Somewhere, he had heard the word *forum*. It suggested 'for 'em.' He was for the people, and the name sounded good." So, the Forum became Hayman's new cafeteria.[187]

While Green knew good food when he tasted it, Hayman knew good food because he cooked it. When his family moved to the Kansas City area from Iowa, his mother became ill, so ten-year-old Clarence took over the kitchen. He knew what it was like to be poor with a rapacious appetite; thus, he learned to expand modest food amounts and ingredients to create terrific meals. At the age of seventeen, Hayman worked as William Rockhill Nelson's farmhand, but he became the cook one day, because he was left "alone at the house and made biscuit and pie for Nelson, an enthusiastic eater," as Hayman's biographer recalled.[188] After leaving domestic service, Hayman traveled to gain restaurant experience before returning to Kansas City in 1911.

With barely $300, Hayman initially started with a diner and then with a lunch counter chain, working in partnership with Clem T. Templin. They tried to open a Forum Cafeteria at Tenth Street and Grand Boulevard (then Grand Avenue) in the Lathrop Building's basement, but it failed. Hayman and Templin did not give up. Instead, in 1918, they incorporated "Forum

A Forum Cafeteria menu from the *Kansas City Star* (November 11, 1940). *From www. newspapers.com.*

Cafeterias of America" to bring in outside investment.[189] Their ground-floor cafeteria at 1220 Grand Boulevard opened in 1921 and was a success, although Templin moved on to other ventures. Hayman trained managers personally until they were equipped to manage a new Forum Cafeteria; three were in operation by 1929, and the chain expanded to St. Louis.[190]

Many recall the Forum at 1212 Main Street, a long-surviving cafeteria downtown. Advertised as Kansas City's first air-conditioned cafeteria, it was beautiful, with a fountain and mezzanine seating that allowed diners to people watch as they ate plates of fried whiting with macaroni and cheese, stuffed creole peppers and rice and roast chicken with mashed potatoes.

The Forum's popularity and egalitarian nature, at least for White people, made it a target of desegregation demonstrations. In July 1960, repeated attempts were made by NAACP members to eat at numerous Kansas City cafeterias—they were rebuffed.[191] Myron Green quietly eliminated segregation, but the Forum held out. Tactics that likely helped persuade the company to integrate, aside from the passage of the Civil Rights Act of 1964, were those deployed by Fellowship House and their multiracial lunchtime gatherings (see chapter 5). When Fellowship House members Lucile Bluford and Virginia Oldham visited the Forum and took their place in line, Bluford (Black) was refused service, but Oldham (White) calmly filled her tray, went with Bluford to find a table and they both sat down and shared their meal, ignoring stares.[192]

When Clarence Miles Hayman Jr. assumed leadership of Forum Cafeterias in the late 1960s, downtown commerce was threatened by suburban development. To remain competitive, in 1969, Forum Restaurants Inc. joined forces with Waid's, a family-owned restaurant chain, and Berbiglia, a liquor store chain. The company opened Forums in shopping centers, including some out of state. A fast-changing culinary landscape posed challenges, however. Consumers rejected cafeterias in favor of fast food and food courts, steakhouse chains and all-you-can-eat buffets. Hayman Jr. recognized the proverbial "writing on the wall" and shuttered the Forum at 1212 Main Street sometime between late 1976 and 1977. From that date to the mid-1980s, shopping mall cafeterias also saw declines in sales, and Forum was soon gone forever.

Putsch's

Most cafeterias were situated downtown when Virginia and Justus "Jud" Putsch opened their cafeteria in 1947 at 4638 Wyandotte Street on the Country Club Plaza, around the corner from Putsch's 210 (see chapter 5).[193] Jud grew up helping his parents, William and Nellie, run Bluebird Cafeteria at 3215 Troost Avenue after his family moved to Kansas City in 1924. Initially, Jud expressed little interest in the restaurant business, leaving for the University of Missouri and then Harvard to earn his MBA. He nonetheless returned home with his wife, Virginia, in 1940, after his mother had passed away and his father had become ill. Together, they ran the Bluebird until Jud entered the navy during World War II. Virginia ran the cafeteria on her own until his return. At that point, they sold the Bluebird.[194]

Putsch's Cafeteria catered less to shoppers and businessmen on lunch break; instead, it met the needs of families from the Plaza neighborhoods. Its aesthetic was modern, in contrast to the old-fashioned grandeur of downtown cafeterias. "A S-shaped sofa that seats 50 is part of the dazzling decor that makes Putsch's Cafeteria a favorite place for families to dine in Kansas City," read a postcard. Another postcard noted the "striking California modern architecture, wrought-iron murals, and extensive use of greenery and driftwood."

Part of what made Putsch's Cafeteria successful was the care that Virginia took when ensuring their employees' well-being. Mary Sanchez, whose father was Putsch's 210's chef, recalled magical Christmas parties that Virginia organized every year for each restaurant the Putsches owned. She ensured "no child was ever left out. And no child ever received the same gift twice." Such gestures made for loyal employees, who were eager to please customers with excellent food and service.[195]

Virginia and Jud expanded, opening a second cafeteria in 1953 at 300 West Forty-Seventh Street, Putsch's Coffee House in 1959 at 333 West Forty-Seventh Street and, when the west end of the same building became available, Putsch's Sidewalk Café in 1967. In 1971, at the height of their

Putsch's Cafeteria, circa the 1950s. *Photographs courtesy of Rebekah Putsch and the Putsch family.*

restaurant fame, the couple sold their business to Montgomery Ward, who continued expanding, including Putsch's Cafeterias at Metcalf South Mall and Ward Parkway Shopping Center (eventually Ward Parkway Mall). However, as food courts became popular, Putsch's Cafeterias slowly began to close. A long-surviving Putsch's Cafeteria at Ward Parkway Mall closed in 1993.

A resurgence of nostalgia for the old-fashioned cafeteria line, with friendly servers and expert cooks dishing up plates of comfort food, has made the name "Putsch's" resonate with Kansas Citians who associate the Plaza's golden age with a time when businesses were local, the food was made from scratch and all manner of gustatory tastes were accounted for.

FROM LUNCH WAGONS TO LUNCH COUNTERS: AGNOS, SANDERSON'S AND NICHOLS

Like many modest entrepreneurs, Clarence M. Hayman started with a lunch counter, a cheap way to begin in the restaurant industry. By placing customers (initially, only men) in a long row on swivel stools within the reach of one or, at most, two waiters (initially, only men), labor costs were minimized and space for customers was maximized. Although lunch was typically the busiest time for service, many lunch counters stayed open twenty-four hours a day.

Agnos Lunch Wagon and Sandwich Shop

The lunch counter evolved from the lunch wagon, rather like a nineteenth-century food truck. In Kansas City, John A. Agnos and his family owned and operated the city's best-remembered lunch wagons. These southern Greek immigrants relied heavily on jazz clubs, most famously the Reno Club, for patrons. During the 1930s, Kansas City trumpeter Richard Smith remembered it "stacked high with liver, pig snoots and ears, hog maws, fish, chicken, and pork tenderloins." One grabbed a sandwich and squeezed back in, "past the hustlers, grifters, solicitors, and off-duty musicians," to find a seat near the bandstand before the next set began.[196]

As tougher regulations were imposed on vendors who competed with powerful restaurants for customers, successful lunch wagon owners invested in brick-and-mortar operations that offered the same food.

Agnos Lunch Wagons changed to Agnos Sandwich Shops, including one located at Twelfth and Forest Streets, where an Agnos horse-drawn lunch wagon had once parked. These were among the last places in Kansas City where people could order brain, pig ear and pig snout (often called snoot) sandwiches—with lots of horseradish and hot sauce.

Sanderson's Lunch

In terms of longevity, let's vicariously step into Sanderson's Lunch at 104 East Eighth Street. In 1914, William Burk Sanderson, a cook, bought his employer's business, Alexander's Lunch, and changed its name to Sanderson's.[197] From 1914 until his passing in 1974, next to nothing changed. In a twelve-foot-by-sixty-foot space—a space so tiny that supplies had to be stored next door—Burk and his mother, Lena, ran a brisk business. Over the decades, other lunch counters closed, but Sanderson's basked in a nostalgic glow and transported patrons to another age.

"He was a very tall man, proper-like, always in a white dress shirt with suspenders," Charles Broomfield recalled of Burk Sanderson. "His mom was a fixture, too. Always seated there at the cash register," he continued.[198] Burk was taciturn, but Lena called all the regulars by name and never feared a confrontation with an unruly customer. "Burk is the official owner. But she runs the place, and she runs him," Alberta Constant observed.[199] Lena started helping when Burk fought in World War I, and when he was drafted for World War II and stationed at Knob Noster, Missouri, she was there to take over again.

Sanderson's was not the proverbial "greasy spoon." Burk cared about quality, and his reputation for excellent meals put him above the competition. He briefly expanded to three locations by the 1920s: 311 East Ninth Street, 19 East Fifth Street and at the original location, although after World War II, only the original location remained. Open twenty-four hours a day, seven days a week (except for Christmas), Sanderson's specialized in all manner of dishes.

While many adored the "Elmer," a burger cooked on a griddle under a lid to trap moisture and melt cheese, Sanderson's specialized in labor-intensive meals that replaced a working person's home-cooked meals. The standouts included spaghetti with huge meatballs and "hot chops for Popeye" (code for breaded tenderloin, mashed potatoes and spinach). By the late 1970s, Sanderson's was one of the few cheap eateries in Kansas City that still sold

An appetizing breakfast menu, featuring cream waffles with honey. For lunch today, featuring Roast Loin of Pork with Cranberry Sauce, Baked Swift's Premium Ham with Potato Salad, Warrensburg Sausage and Fried Sweet Potatoes. Equally good evening meals, and a superior 24-hour short order service at all three locations.

Sanderson's Lunch
104 East 8th   311 East 9th
            19 East 5th

Sanderson's advertisement from the *Kansas City Star* (November 1924). *From www. newspapers.com.*

from-scratch specialties, like braised ox tails in gravy. People willingly lined up outside in all types of weather to wait until they could finally enter the restaurant, then stand along the mirrored wall and wait again until it was their turn to take a seat at the counter.

Burk willed Sanderson's to Elva Wilson, a waitress and Burk's companion; Irene Blodgett; and Jimmie Fox, the main cook. Within a couple of years of their ownership, Wilson and Blodgett were too frail to continue, and the restaurant was sold in 1979 to Arthur W. Lamb, a friend of Blodgett's daughter.[200] Having served over three generations, Sanderson's succumbed to downtown blight, as well as its ancient building that was riddled with problems. Lamb had no choice but to move, and from 1981 until 1984, Sanderson's operated at 3800 Main Street. Lamb then sold Sanderson's to Suppasan Inc., which moved it to 7907 State Line Road in 1999, but it failed to thrive, and this icon was bulldozed in 2000.[201]

"People are the same," speculated Sanderson's former waitress, Vanessa Coots, as she tried to account for the old lunch counter's appeal. "In the end, they're all looking for some comfort, whether it be in the meatloaf and mashed potatoes, the company of stool mates or just a friendly place to sit for a while and let the steam from their coffee cup warm their souls." Sanderson's, Rest in Peace.

Nichols Lunch

As the Agnos family established their lunch wagons, Foti Nicolopoulos (sometimes Nicolopolis) sailed from Greece and ended up working in

Kansas City's railyards. Foti anglicized his name to Frank Nichols and left the rail job to start a lunch counter.[202] Writing about why a restaurant was often the route to economic security for Greek Americans, John Mariani speculated that it had to do with how many Greek men worked for the railroads, where they were inspired by the rail dining cars.[203] Frank operated lunch counters in various places starting in 1921, but his best-remembered location was at the present-day intersection of Southwest Trafficway and Thirty-Ninth Street. All of Frank's locations were tiny, and he stuck to lunch counter mainstays, including tenderloins, brain sandwiches and chili. Frank's door was located at the streetcar turnaround for downtown. That traffic sustained his business, as did a nickel slot machine that was initially placed near the front door.[204]

The slot machine aside, Nichols Lunch did not endure for eighty-five years without an iron-clad work ethic and multigenerational commitment to a dream. With the help of Frank's wife, Bessie, and their children, the family operated the business twenty-four hours a day, six days a week. The space expanded from twenty-four to forty seats, and in 1996, it was seven times larger.

The food remained straightforward, with an all-day breakfast being the biggest draw, including the Lil' Abner with pork chops and eggs. It was also purportedly the last Kansas City restaurant to offer what had been a beloved combination back in the day: brains and scrambled eggs. Customers depended on Nichols Lunch for excellent coffee, especially when sobering up after a night carousing. Frank kept some reign on sobriety in the early days by refusing to put soft drinks on the menu; he was nervous that if he did so, patrons would spike their drinks with their own liquor.[205]

When Frank passed away in 1962, his son Jimmie and Jimmie's wife, Eva, assumed leadership of the restaurant without any disruption in its operations or work ethic. Nonetheless, they grew anxious that they could not keep up with new restaurant trends when it came to metrics and supply chains, so they sold the restaurant in 1976 to a business operating truck stops—only to watch the restaurant be nearly destroyed by poor remote management. When the restaurant went back on the market, Jimmie and Eva bought it back, this time assured that their old-fashioned management methods appealed to Kansas Citians who were unimpressed by dining fads and gimmicks.

When Jimmie passed in 1996, his nephew Michael Bay assumed ownership, keeping the same low prices and welcoming all types of people. The restaurant never excluded the intoxicated, the drag queens from nearby

A Nichols Lunch advertisement from the *Kansas City Star* (November 25, 1970). *From www. newspapers.com.*

Missie B's, insomniacs, delivery truck operators on the graveyard shift, broke students or neighborhood people who depended on Nichols Lunch for one or more meals a day. "The irony of Nichols' longevity," Charles Ferruzza speculated, was that "by serving cheap and unfussy homestyle food, this greasy spoon marched right into the twenty-first century, unlike most of the city's fancy, upscale restaurants."[206]

Nichols Lunch finally closed because of skyrocketing wholesale prices and other expenses. Bay chose not to raise his own prices to compensate or to buy inferior products. It made more sense to sell. On September 24, 2006, Nichols Lunch served its final patrons, cleaned up and locked its door. Restaurants have come and gone at that address since then, routinely reminding Kansas Citians of what they have lost.

A BURGER AND A MALTED: KATZ DRUGS

Many Kansas Citians patronized drugstore grills and soda fountains—chief among them, Katz Drug Company, which was in business from 1914 to 1971. Drugstores entered the soda fountain business due to a belief that soda water's healing properties mimicked natural mineral waters but for a pittance of the price. Terre Haute pharmacist Jacob Bauer started the Liquid Carbonic Acid Manufacturing Company in 1888 by liquifying carbon dioxide and distributing it under pressure in cylinders. Liquid Carbonic's product line included recipes, fruits and syrups that druggists purchased along with soda fountain hardware.[207]

Katz became an icon due to its longevity, ability to sell everything from pets to orchids and, most importantly, the hypnotic effect its cat face logo had on generations of children.

That logo was only part of Isaac and Michael Katz's genius. The two brothers were brought up on the art of the hustle. And from the time that they arrived from present-day Ukraine to St. Paul, Minnesota, and then went on to Kansas City, they worked purposefully and with nothing short of genius to climb the ladder as salesmen.[208]

In 1914, the brothers invested in two confectionery and tobacco stands at Twelfth and McGee Streets and Eighth Street and Grand Boulevard (then Avenue). Instead of seeing wartime restrictions as problematic, they leveraged them for business, including paying a one-cent tobacco tax themselves and proudly posting that fact in their windows: "Katz Pays the Tax." When all retail stores were ordered to close at 6:00 p.m. to conserve fuel, the Katz brothers rebranded their confectionary-tobacco store as a drugstore to stay open later. They hired pharmacists, and when suspicious officials came by to check, there were the pharmacists, compounding medicines.[209]

By 1929, Katz was a powerful chain, and its branches featured a soda fountain and grill. Its popular treats included everything from cherry phosphates and root beer floats to banana splits and the Imperial chocolate soda. Unlike smaller operations, Katz expanded its savory food selections beyond sandwiches and burgers. In the 1950s, one could order weekly "blue-plate specials" for fifty-nine cents, including roast turkey and pot pies.

Given its visibility, the drugstore chain became a target for sit-ins to desegregate lunch counters. When, in 1948, Edna Griffin, her daughter and friends were refused service at a Des Moines, Iowa, Katz Drugs, Griffin organized boycotts and sit-ins. She also took Katz to court for criminal and

Katz Drugs at Tenth and Minnesota Streets in Kansas City, Kansas. *Courtesy of Missouri Valley Special Collections, Kansas City Public Library (Kansas City, MO).*

civil charges.[210] In 1951, St. Louis CORE (Committee of Racial Equality) targeted the St. Louis downtown Katz lunch counter. Margaret Dagen and fellow CORE member Wanda Penny visited Earl Katz, Katz's board chairman, and sought his backing to allow two interracial customers to visit Katz "on a regular basis, every week, and be served." Katz executives in Kansas City "negotiated integration of Katz lunch counters throughout the region," Dagen recalled, and shortly thereafter, discrimination was forbidden at all thirty-eight Katz outlets in Missouri, Oklahoma, Kansas and Iowa.[211]

By 1970, Katz operated fifty-plus stores in five states, generating $100 million in sales and employing over three thousand people. However, nationwide drugstore conglomerates were increasingly competitive, so Katz merged with Skaggs Drug Company in 1971, and at that point—to the dismay of child and adult alike—Katz logos around Kansas City were dismantled, as were the soda fountains that have since gone down in history for both their nostalgia and Civil Rights battles.

SOUL FOOD INSTITUTIONS: RUBY'S AND MAXINE'S FINE FOODS

Ruby's Cafe at 1506 Brooklyn Avenue and Maxine's Fine Foods at 3041 Benton Avenue arguably had Kansas City's most loyal patrons. These modest businesses welcomed people from all races and walks of life, and their proprietors, women who proudly called themselves cooks, not chefs, understood that the power of harmony and peace resided in meals people shared in intimate spaces, without the distractions of fancy décor.

Ruby's Café

From 1952 to 2001, Ruby's was run by Ruby Watson McIntyre, who had been cooking for most of her life. Biographical facts regarding McIntyre's life are obscure and sometimes conflicting. She was born in Lexington, Tennessee, in 1920, and there, she and her family sharecropped on a plantation. Around the age of five, Ruby learned to cook for her employer, Effie Howe. As she told the story to a reporter, Eric Adler, "Everybody else went into the field and picked cotton. I stayed in the house and did all the cooking and housework, too."[212]

In an interview with William Jewell College students, McIntyre explained that she was eight when her family moved to Kansas City. She started cooking for money "by selling pies out of the back of a car." In another interview with Jan Smith, McIntyre said that in the 1940s, she and her first husband briefly ran a diner in Olathe, Kansas. A few years later, a new highway took that spot, so she moved her equipment to a "hole in the wall" at Fifteenth Street and Brooklyn Avenue. Once there, she cooked for a friend who was working at a nearby laundry. Soon, she took dinner to all the laundry workers. Cooking on a four-burner stove with just two tables, one booth and three stools, McIntyre began serving coffee, rolls and hamburgers. Then she added beans and greens, and from there, she designed a full Southern-style menu. She married Otis Johnson in 1976.[213]

McIntyre cooked, as she put it, "with [her] right hand and brain," shunning measurements. "I do it all by myself. I just enjoy cooking. It's not a chore to me," she explained to Joyce Smith. "I love [people] and feed them; they can't get mad."[214] Indeed, McIntyre was a peacemaker; using food and her café, she challenged Kansas City's ugly race relations problems. She joined Ed Chasteen's Kansas City HateBusters in 1988 to expose hate while seeking avenues to racial harmony. McIntyre's achievements resulted in an invitation that she and twenty-five other HateBusters received in 1997 to visit the White House. As she related the story, "When I went to Washington, D.C....and cooked for 350 people, that's my high point. A little woman like me invited up there by President Clinton."[215]

While "Mama Ruby," as she was affectionately known, exuded love and peace, by necessity, she had a steel core. "NOTICE: This is not Burger King. You get it my way, or you don't get the son-of-a-bitch at all," warned a sign in the entryway. Many short-term closings of Ruby's were the results of misfortunes that

Ruby Watson McIntyre. *Author's collection.*

would have left other business owners defeated, but in all cases, McIntyre pulled through and, with grace, accepted help and donations from patrons. A restaurant robbery in the mid-1970s left her with broken legs, and although the police arrived within minutes, the damage almost put Ruby out of business. A year later, a car slammed through Ruby's front walls. Patrons stepped in to fundraise and repair damages. A fire in the 1990s closed Ruby's for four months, but funds were raised to not only repair but also remodel and enlarge the building to accommodate one hundred people, two buffets and a parking lot. People kept coming.

The homemade food was indescribably delicious. As Chasteen characterized it, patrons were presented with "wave after wave of mouth-watering foods; salads of every conceivable kind, fried chicken, chicken and dressing, chicken and dumplings, smothered steak, baked ham, catfish, meatloaf, neckbones, minced greens, homemade rolls and cornbread." The dessert table was loaded with "peach and cherry cobbler, sweet potato pie, apple pie, banana pudding, pecan pie, several cakes, and homemade ice cream."[216]

Only poor health could ultimately stop McIntyre, but her spirit and grace live on in people's memories. As tribute to her passing, Joe's Kansas City Barbecue Facebook post summarized how so many felt: "Ruby's Soul Food Restaurant was a righteous and true Kansas City culinary and cultural legend."[217]

Maxine's

Considering Maxine's Fine Foods' tiny size, it must have been a sight when the Kansas City Chiefs and Royals crowded into it. Located near Municipal Stadium, it was an unassuming place.[218] While most were still asleep, Maxine Byrd prepared grits, biscuits, home fries, sausage gravy, breaded pork chops and huge flapjacks. By sunrise, the place was jammed, as regulars took their place at the counter or crammed into the booths to eat up—but not before Byrd had liberally distributed her hugs. Her generosity was legendary. When someone could not pay, Byrd filled out an IOU. "We treat people the way I would want to be treated. Like family," Byrd explained to Carla Labat. "When people are feeling down or just need to get out, they come to Maxine's."[219]

Byrd cooked at many eateries, including a Crown Drugs Lunch Counter, where a customer convinced her to open her own restaurant: "As hard as you work for these people, you ought to be working for yourself," the customer advised.[220] With roughly $300, Byrd bought a building at 3041 Benton Avenue in 1962. She had too little money to turn on the utilities, so her mentor and friend Ollie Gates of Gates Bar-B-Q covered the costs.[221]

Byrd excelled at her breakfast specials and encouraged serious conversation over coffee. The Chiefs' wide receiver Otis Taylor often showed up with Reverend Dr. Charles Briscoe. Both were integral to mitigating flare-ups of race hate that wracked Kansas City in the 1960s and '70s.[222] Recalling those turbulent decades, sportswriter Michael MacCambridge observed that the restaurant's magnetism came from Byrd's "irrepressible" optimism and kindness; her "diner was a haven for not only the Chiefs and the Royals, but also many African American athletes visiting the city."[223]

Byrd was especially close to the Chiefs' linebacker Derrick Thomas, who, along with Michael Tellis, died when his vehicle flipped on a snowy patch of I-435 in 2000. When in town, Thomas always called Byrd on his cellphone, requesting breakfast. "I'd say, 'Where you at?'" Byrd recalled, "And he'd walk through the door with this big smile." Byrd scrambled eggs with rice and cheddar, alongside an order of pancakes with extra syrup.[224]

Singers often commemorate legendary cooks in their lyrics. When it came to Byrd, Hank Williams Jr. did so with "The Last Porkchop" on his 2002 album, *Almeria Club*. Ostensibly "a ribald tune about food, booze, and women," as Timothy Finn characterized it, the song also immortalized

Byrd's cooking.[225] Indeed, Williams did like his "gravy on the side," and his "sausage warm out of the oven." "Sometimes," the lyrics continue, you have to ask yourself, "Why, oh, why did I leave that last porkchop?"

Byrd suffered a stroke in 2002, forcing patrons to confront the fact that no one is immortal and that no restaurant lasts forever. For a time, Byrd's daughter, Velta Campbell, kept Maxine's operating, but ultimately, it closed in 2003. The loss of Maxine's makes Williams Jr.'s refrain more poignant for all those souls who left the café with food still on their plates.

Here from the Start

MEXICAN AMERICAN RESTAURANTS

From 1762 to 1800, Kawsmouth was part of Spain's *Nueva España*. From that time forward, the area's culinary heritage would always be indebted to Hispanic and Native peoples. Beans with game, jerky, wild herbs and precious chili peppers represented the melding of cultures that happened along the Santa Fe and Chisolm Trails, when wagons camped and a pot was slung over a campfire. Kansas Citians have never rejected their love of spicy, chili-laden food.

Mexican restaurants opened in Kansas City as a result of the railyard's presence and meatpacking. Recruits from Michoacán, Jalisco and Guanajuato, Mexico, guarded their food traditions, improvising both ingredients and cooking methods as necessary. The Mexican Revolution increased immigration to the area, with newcomers settling the West Side and Kansas City, Kansas's Argentine and Armourdale districts. Mexican culinary identity was reinforced by racism and discrimination. Despite eating chili and tamales (often from vendors in the early days), most non-Mexican Kansas Citians had no knowledge of or interest in visiting tiny eateries that catered to Mexican people. For decades, Mexican residents relied on Mexican groceries to supply much of their food and sundries, particularly tortillas, chorizo, menudo, cheese and tamales.

As it does in many first-generation immigrant communities, the hospitality industry became an alternative route to economic stability for the Mexican community in Kansas City. For Mexicans who opted to work in hotel kitchens and restaurants, the majority settled in Missouri because liberal liquor laws generated brisk business for establishments that depended on liquor sales. On the Kansas side, families could turn their homes into small groceries and restaurants. Some became increasingly well known to the wider metro area, due to their longevity and excellent food. The restaurants in this chapter survived for generations and shaped the city's culinary DNA in ways that remain evident in grocery stores and many Mexican restaurants. It honors restaurateurs who introduced the city to the delicious flavors for which Mexican food is renowned.

LAYING THE FOUNDATION:
EL NOPAL AND LALA'S ORIGINAL MEXICAN FOOD

Opening in 1930, El Nopal was reputedly the area's first restaurant to consciously introduce a wider Kansas City audience to Mexican food.[226] Ignacio and Eulalia "Lala" Alvarez Infante turned part of their home into a restaurant, but instead of serving the more expected barbecue or fried chicken that were popular with these types of Depression-era eateries, Lala focused on Mexican specialties. Located at 416 West Thirteenth Street in Kansas City, Missouri, El Nopal comprised two small dining rooms. The family lived upstairs.[227]

Ignacio managed El Nopal while working two jobs, including one as a Muehlebach Hotel waiter, while Lala and her older children cooked, waited tables and cleaned. El Nopal rose to such prominence that by 1945, it was featured in WHB *Swing*'s "Kansas City Ports of Call," where the reviewer urged readers to seek it out. "We recommend what they call the 'combination,' a plate of tortillas, enchiladas, tacos, and beans or rice."[228] Most Kansas Citians loved tamales and chili (popularized by Jim's Tamales carts and Dixon's Chili Parlor), and they were well acquainted with beans and cornbread. As such, many readily took to Lala's Mexican preparation of these inexpensive staples, her spices adding spark to an often-bland diet.

While it would be impossible to pinpoint how the "Kansas City" taco came to be, folding seasoned ground meat into corn tortillas, tooth-picking them shut, and deep-frying them, that was precisely how the Infante family prepared their tacos, wrote Suzanne Infante Lozano. The fried tacos were then opened and topped with lettuce, hand-chopped by Ignacio, salsa and—unusual—a sprinkling of grated parmesan cheese. It was a pragmatic option, given the proximity of the Italian immigrants who worked alongside Mexicans in the West Bottoms and who produced the cheese for their own

Lala's Original Mexican Food menu. *Courtesy of Suzanne Infante Lozano, Josephine, Henry, Michael Infante and Delores Salazar.*

restaurants' and family's needs, wrote Jose Ralet when he interviewed Jean Silva Miller about growing up in her parents' Spanish Gardens restaurant in Argentine, Kansas City, Kansas.[229]

As El Nopal's popularity grew, the Infante family moved its location to Fourteenth Street and Pennsylvania Avenue, but Kansas City's fast-changing infrastructure, including the construction of Southwest Trafficway, resulted in the family selling the property and opening Lala's Original Mexican Food at Thirty-Third and Troost Avenue in 1966. It lasted only a short time, as Lala had tired of both cooking and operating her restaurant. She turned to what we might call restaurant consulting, or teaching others to create her signature flavors, recalled Suzanne Infante Lozano.[230]

Jeannie Barrera, whose family still operates the Claycomo restaurant El Sombrero, remembered when Lala came to work for them in 1964, helping the struggling business attract patrons. She "brought Mom and Dad her recipes and entrusted us to keep this great food going," Barrera explained.[231] The Barrera family still uses Lala's recipes, honoring her contributions. Lozano, when asked what dishes she loved most from her mother's repertoire, praised her mother's pork chunks in her burritos and chili and her Spanish rice. While Lala made wonderful tamales once a week, when they ran out, they were out. "Tamales were hard to make quickly," Lozano explained, and her mother found them troublesome, no matter how much patrons craved them.

BUILDING A FAMILY LEGACY: MARGARITA'S, LOS IBARRAS AND THE RED BULL

Margarita's Mexican Restaurant

While the Infante family ran El Nopal, a woman named Guadalupe opened a Mexican restaurant called Lupe's in 1942 at 618 West Forty-Eighth Street on the Country Club Plaza. Sadly, Lupe's and its owner have largely been lost to history. What we know is that Lupe's took over what had been Kamen's Market and that Lupe's closed when the space was then leased by Marguerite V. Bailey sometime between 1947 and 1948. Lupe's short advertisements indicated that the restaurant offered enchiladas, tamales, chili and tacos, but due to the restaurant's lack of air conditioning, it was closed for a month or two each summer.

We know a bit more about Margarita Bailey's Mexican restaurant thanks to C.W. Gusewelle's restaurant column. Bailey grew up in West Central Mexico. In Kansas City, her husband worked for the railroads while she, assisted by Ernestina Diaz, ran her restaurant. Margarita's Mexican Restaurant featured Swiss enchiladas, a dish thought to have originated in Mexico City.[232] Bailey filled her homemade corn tortillas with cheese, shredded chicken and green pepper, topping them with sour cream to resemble the Swiss Alps. Gusewelle also praised Bailey's chiles rellenos con picadillo, made delicious by the addition of currants and chopped pecans. With advance notice, Margarita's also prepared chicken mole and arroz valenciana for a loyal clientele.[233]

Betty and Gus Ibarra: Los Ibarras and the Red Bull

By 1968, when Bailey had retired and the building at 618 West Forty-Eighth Street had been leased to Augustine "Gus" Ibarra, Mexican food's popularity had grown, due to not only Guadalupe, Marguerite Bailey and Lala Infante but also Gus and Betty Ibarra. Los Ibarras, reputedly Johnson County's first Mexican restaurant, opened in 1960 near Seventy-Ninth Street and Metcalf Avenue.[234] Success led the couple to open a larger restaurant at 7700 West Sixty-Third Street shortly thereafter.

Los Ibarras "is immensely popular, and reservations are absolutely necessary," counseled Gusewelle. The recipes came both from Gus's mother, Elvira, a native of Torreon, Coahuila, Mexico, as well as Gus himself. Particularly distinctive was the family recipe for fideo, toasted vermicelli simmered with tomatoes, Mexican spices and chicken broth. The gordo, a "bun of tortilla dough, fried and sliced, filled with beans, beef, cheese, onions, lettuce and Spanish rice," is also delicious, wrote Gusewelle.[235]

The Ibarra children worked in the restaurant, and Gus's brother, Arturo, also joined the business. By 1964, the two brothers had opened Los Ibarras 2 in Claycomo, Missouri, catering to workers at the nearby Ford plant and to Northlanders. After Gus and Betty divorced, the Claycomo restaurant became Ibarra Red Bull, and the brothers began expanding their business, thus exposing wider swaths of suburban Kansas City to Mexican food. A Red Bull opened at 7520 West Sixty-Third Street in Overland Park with the Red Bull Pen, a private club that allowed diners to drink alcohol with their meals (Kansas liquor laws at that time prohibited alcohol unless it was served in a private club), and at 5410 Northeast Antioch Road in the Kansas City Northland, which eventually replaced the Claycomo Restaurant. Sustaining the Plaza's reputation for offering visitors a Mexican restaurant option, the brothers leased the 618 West Forty-Eighth Street address when Bailey closed Margarita's in 1968.

The Ibarras greeted their patrons personally and escorted them to their tables. Part of their success also came from their restaurants' atmosphere. In an era before fast-casual and Mexican chains, Red Bull felt like a special occasion restaurant, with waitstaff in bow ties and candles on the tables to add atmosphere. Nonetheless, the food was affordable, and some might say addictive, especially the sopapillas. The pillow-soft fried dough came to the table with a shaker of cinnamon and honey kept warm by a votive candle flickering underneath its little metal pot. "The Red Bull was the first Mexican restaurant I remember eating at as a child—and the first sopapillas I ever had," recalled Mark Stahl, a memory that many resonate with, including this author.

Between 1970 and 1980, the number of Mexican restaurants in the area increased to more than eighty, many of them national chains, such as Taco Bell. Competition was keen and so was corporate investment. The Plaza

A Red Bull advertisement from the *Kansas City Star* (Mary 31, 1973). *From www.newspapers.com.*

Denise Ibarra Hamilton saved her dad's sopapilla paraphernalia from the Red Bull for use in her Torreon Mexican Restaurant, still in operation near the Ibarras' original restaurant in Overland Park, Kansas. *Author's photograph.*

Red Bull location closed shortly before the highly anticipated arrival of Gilbert-Robinson's Annie's Santa Fe, which opened in 1974. The Sixty-Third Street Ibarra Red Bull restaurant was sold by 1975, and the longest-surviving Ibarra Red Bull on Antioch Road was gone by the early 1980s. The Ibarra brothers left restauranting behind for good. Nonetheless, Denise Ibarra Hamilton, Gus and Betty's youngest child, continues to operate Torreon in Overland Park, the restaurant that Betty started after she and Gus divorced. The fideo, gorditas, and the sopapillas remain on Torreon's menu—the recipes unchanged and beloved by Torreon's loyal clientele, some of whom remember Los Ibarras and the magic of their first time eating Mexican food.

AN ARMOURDALE INSTITUTION: MOLINA'S

No discussion of Mexican restaurants in Kansas City would be complete without highlighting Molina's at 401 Kansas Avenue in Armourdale, Kansas City, Kansas, an establishment that Kansas City's favorite broadcaster, Walt Bodine, described as a "lovable joint" filled with "wonderful smells."[236] It opened in 1948, when Bonifacio "Barney" and Senobia Molina bought a grocery store from the Bukaty family and decided to make Mexican food for carryout. Barney and Senobia were newcomers, having moved from Indiana to Kansas City, Kansas, where Barney initially worked in meatpacking. Senobia's carryout business proved to be so popular that she offered classes for women who wanted to learn how to cook Mexican food.[237] The Molina family lived frugally and saved their money—a wise decision, given that Armourdale and the West Bottoms were underwater for days when the devastating Flood of 1951 rang a death knell for the stockyard and meatpacking way of life. Instead of relocating, Barney and Senobia used their $5,000 in savings to rebuild the business.[238]

The couple retired to Overland Park but continued to lease their store to others, including Jesse C. and Ruth Rodriguez, who began running Molina's in 1969 and likely bought it after Barney Molina passed away in 1980.[239] Ruth and Jesse carried on the grocery store's and eatery's traditions, specializing in house-made chorizo, enchilada sauce, menudo and a variety of staples, including nopales and shrimp powder. When they retired, they sold the business to Nick and Mary Rachel Vega (now Mary Rachel Rocha), and during this period, Molina's grew into a Kansas City favorite.[240]

In its third generation, Molina's continued serving an array of foods but this time, with the Vega family's signature stamp. Nick Vega's taco and enchilada sauces were so popular that customers who had moved away planned a visit to Molina's to stock up before heading home. "Their sauces and spices were outstanding," wrote Dennis Shmania, whose family had moved to Indianapolis. The tortillas were likewise "to die for. We had a cooler filled with them because you couldn't come close to anything like them in Indianapolis."[241] On weekends, "a trip to Molina's meant a piping hot bowl of menudo served with a pile of fresh, steaming corn tortillas, a side plate with freshly diced onions, juicy lemon wedges, thick-cut Mexican oregano and spicy chili flakes. Pour the condiments on your bowl of menudo, sprinkle a little salt in your corn tortilla, roll it up and enjoy the experience," remembered Jesse John Vega Sr., Nick Vega's son.[242] Jesse's older brother, Michael, cut up twenty cases of tripe in anticipation of selling out of the classic hangover soup long before Sunday afternoon.

Molina's tamales were also popular. Jesse remembered vividly that their tamale machine "produced three-bite pork tamales that would sell out as fast as they were made," while the cooks, including the main cook, Maria, prepared "big, fat handmade pork chili tamales full of meaty chunks of spicy chili-slathered pork."

After the Vegas divorced, Mary and her second husband opened La Mexicana Express in the City Market while Nick continued, with the help of his staff and children, to run Molina's. Jesse described his father's offerings as "Tex-Mex," based on the food of his childhood in Bastrop, Texas. A steam table stood at the ready, replete with carne asada, pork carnitas and chicken, chorizo or nopales burritos. Molina's tacos were stuffed with seasoned meat, closed with a toothpick and

"Big Nick" Vega. Jesse recounted about his dad, "He had a tireless work ethic, but he was also an authentic Texas desperado who had 'The El Paso Kid' tattooed across his right fist. Nobody messed with Big Nick." *Portrait courtesy of Jesse John Vega Sr.*

deep-fried, lending a distinctive Kansas City feel to the otherwise Tex-Mex menu. The pinto beans, another specialty, simmered for hours before they were seasoned, smashed with lard and transformed into a creamy concoction that "spread beautifully over a hot flour tortilla," reminisced Jesse.

Molina's popularity came from its commitment to preserving a family culinary heritage, one that set it apart from generic Mexican franchises. Even today, Kansas Citians still pine for a Molina's replacement. Sharon Rains inquired hopefully in a 2020 Facebook post, "Does anyone know if there is any place to find products like theirs, or are they open in another location?" While she received seventy-six comments with some suggestions, most respondents simply lamented Molina's closure.

LAS PALMAS MEXICAN RESTAURANT

The idea of opening a Mexican restaurant came somewhat late in Guadalupe Bribiesca Garcia's career, and likely, Las Palmas was as much a manifestation of her cultural diplomacy as it was a way to earn a living.

In 1926, she and her husband, Primitivo, emigrated with their children from Salamanca, Mexico, to Kansas City, fleeing religious persecution and the Mexican Revolution. Upon their arrival, both were integral to the Guadalupe Center at Twenty-Third and Jarboe Streets in Kansas City, Missouri, where Guadalupe took up organizing and event planning. She helped arrange the Gran Fiestas that introduced a wider Kansas City audience to Mexican culture while also working with the National Folk Heritage program in Washington, D.C., during the 1930s.[243]

Guadalupe also cooked for the Fred Harvey Company at Union Station, expanding her culinary repertoire.[244] Her love of cooking and desire to share the fruits of her labor with others made her a natural for the restaurant business. "Dona Lupe, why are you always giving away your food? You should set up a restaurant," urged Fernando Oberlin, the Mexican consul in Kansas City.[245] Eventually, she acted on his advice. As she and her family were driving down Prospect Avenue one day, her grandson Donald Quinn II recalled, they spotted a potential location, an old meatpacking warehouse. After its renovation in 1948, Guadalupe opened Las Palmas there, at 4551 Prospect Avenue.

Critical to the restaurant's success was the family's musical prominence. Primitivo played classical guitar, and Guadalupe, a contralto, sang at the dedication of Municipal Auditorium in 1936. The Garcia children, Victoria, Lupe (later Sister Ann Victoria, SCL) and Carlos, were known as the Las Palmas Trio and performed locally and regionally while assisting their mother with Guadalupe Center's talent shows.[246] The prominence of the Garcia family raised the new Las Palmas Restaurant's profile, and within six months—the timeframe that Guadalupe had given herself to either profit or close the business—the restaurant became a Kansas City culinary destination.

When Guadalupe wished to retire, the family closed the Prospect restaurant. For two years, there was no Las Palmas. During this time, her daughter Victoria Garcia Quinn and her husband, Donald, built a new location in the Santa Fe Shopping Center, which was opened in 1968.

Donald designed the restaurant's interiors, making it fan "out like a rounded triangle, and in the middle was a large pole decorated as a palm tree," recalled Victoria and Donald Quinn's daughter Kathy. Divided into three sections, green, tan and orange, with leather chairs to match each section, patrons dined while listening to live classical guitar.[247]

Gusto characterized both Victoria and Las Palmas, according to *Kansas City Star* reporter Jane P. Fowler. Victoria saw tacos, enchiladas and frijoles as

A grand opening flyer for Las Palmas. *Courtesy of the Garcia-Quinn family.*

"the essence of celebration," foods typical throughout Mexico and the stuff of festivals. The restaurant also specialized in dishes from Guanajuato. "We don't tone it down," Victoria explained when asked about Mexican food and its heat. "We cook it like they do in our home state, with the real spices that are imported." While patrons loved standard offerings, like chili con queso and enchiladas, its signature specialties were particularly noteworthy, including costillas Mexicana, pork short ribs braised in a sauce of many chili varieties. Indeed, Las Palmas is best remembered for its pork dishes, including chili con carne, made with refried beans and tender pork chunks.

The deaths of Guadalupe Garcia in June 1977 and Victoria in August 2017 were losses for Kansas City. Throughout their lives, the two served as Kansas City's Mexican American cultural leaders, to the extent that Guadalupe's name is engraved on the Women's Leadership Fountain at Ninth Street and The Paseo Boulevard. Las Palmas itself closed in 1978, but as social media fans of the restaurant can attest, the flavors persist in people's memories.

A Distinctive Heritage

ITALIAN AMERICAN RESTAURANTS

Readers will know from previous chapters that some lost Kansas City restaurants were owned by Italian families, especially the steakhouses. The restaurants in this chapter, however, were consciously styled as Italian eateries, where patrons from outside Italian enclaves would expect to see a variety of dishes and products that they associated with Italian cooking, even if, initially, they were unfamiliar with products such as olive oil and ricotta.

Most Italian immigrants in Kansas City came from agricultural backgrounds and settled here with a knowledge of foodstuffs that surpassed those of many other settlers. Many immediately found a livelihood in wholesale food marketing and production, running stands and brick-and-mortar businesses clustered in the City Market and the North End (today's Columbus Park).[248] They supplied everything from cannoli shells to imported anchovies and olives, initially catering to their own community's culinary needs before their popularity expanded to include larger numbers of Kansas Citians. As such, it is difficult to date when Kansas City's very first Italian restaurant opened. One early mention of Matteo Pecoraro's Restaurant in the North End dates to 1908.[249]

The restaurants in this chapter consciously catered to a wide patron base, were often run by several generations of the same family and put in place culinary expectations for Italian cuisine that still resonate. In short, they help us understand what "Italian food" meant to early twentieth-century Kansas Citians who had little familiarity with it, and they help us better understand how the cuisine evolved to feature a variety of Italian-inspired dishes that many Kansas Citians have come to expect today.

LAYING THE FOUNDATION: LASALA'S, ITALIAN GARDENS AND IL PAGLIACCIO

LaSala's

The southern Italians who made up most of Kansas City's Italian immigrant population were disinclined to assimilate their culinary traditions to the American mainstream. They took it upon themselves to ensure that olive oil and pasta were available and that artisans supplied the community with wine, cheese, bread, pastry and charcuterie. Along with Roma Bakery (initially at 1303 Independence Avenue), Joe LaSala's Sanitary Market was critical to the North End community. He and his family opened LaSala's in 1921 at 910 East Fifth Street. For generations, the business passed from father to son (the family always included either a Joe or an Albert at the head of operations).

After World War II, the grocery industry gradually changed from small businesses to larger chains. While the LaSala family had been selling prepared sandwiches at least as early as the 1930s, their focus shifted away from groceries and toward a deli and restaurant to remain economically viable. Best remembered was the "Poor Boy," although the LaSala family is hazy on how the name came about. While many associate this submarine-style sandwich with New Orleans, a popular version of LaSala's origin story for the sandwich involved a man who came into the shop during the Depression and asked if the grocer could make a sandwich for a poor boy.[250] Both the Poor Boy (four different cold cuts and cheeses) and the Rich Boy (which doubled the meat and cheeses) fed several people. Charles Ferruzza remembered them being the length of a man's forearm, a full loaf of Roma Bakery's sesame seed–studded bread sliced open and piled high. "Hurt-your-mouth" sandwiches, many called them, due to the effort it took to bite through one. A KCUR *Friday Food Critics* caller enthused: "The flavors that come together when you bite into a Poor Boy or a Rich Boy are so perfect. Garlic and spices from the meat, that beautiful Roma bread, mayonnaise, tomato, onion…now, that's a sandwich!"[251]

LaSala's was unpretentious. It became a treasured reminder of once-common neighborhood groceries, with its narrow aisles, fluorescent lights and a long counter where people bought pickled eggs and pigs' feet from glass jars. Along with sandwiches, LaSala's also began offering an array of "comfort food," including chicken breast Romano, lasagna and the ever-popular meatball sub.

In 2013, Albert LaSala and his family closed shop. For eighty-plus years, they had served thousands of Kansas Citians. Now, just memories persist.

Italian Gardens

While LaSala's opened as a neighborhood grocery, Italian Gardens, from its inception, was a restaurant, and arguably, no restaurant epitomized downtown Kansas City's golden age quite like it. Its closure in December 2003 was not met with indifference—no, it was met with a keen sense that the city had lost a piece of itself.

Italian Gardens started under a different name, however. In 1925, two families related by marriage opened Il Trovatore No. 1 at 605–7 Locust Street and Il Trovatore No. 2 at 1300 Walnut Street. The No. 2 location, run by Johnny Abbandonato (anglicized to Bondon) and his sister, Teresa, would go on to become Italian Gardens. Shortly after opening, Johnny's nephew, Frank Lipari, joined the business at the height of the "Roaring Twenties." Then came the Wall Street crash.

However, the Bondons already knew hardship. Johnny's parents had emigrated from Potenza, Basilicata, Italy, where the diet was *cucina povera*, or the food of peasants, and the Bondons knew how to make a lot out of little, making it delicious all the same. Teresa oversaw the kitchen—really the family kitchen, clarified Carl J. DiCapo—where she made ravioli that brought the restaurant praise.[252]

During Prohibition, Lipari and Bondon served "shot beer," where near-beer was served in wide-mouthed bottles, into which one could drop a shot glass (full of bootleg whiskey). "Shot beer usually cost twenty-five cents," wrote DiCapo, "but it ended up costing Johnny and Frank their license." They found a new location at Sixteenth Street and Grand Boulevard and named it Italian Gardens. Teresa oversaw the kitchen. However, the Grand Boulevard address suffered from slow evening traffic, so with the help of a waitress, who loaned Bondon and Lipari $1,500, the restaurant relocated to bustling "Hotel Row," 1110 Baltimore Avenue, in 1933.

Italian Gardens was literally a family affair, with the DiCapos, Berbiglias, Bondons and Liparis joined by various marriages. Critical to the restaurant's success was Carl J. DiCapo's energy and hospitality. He began working there in 1953, when his brother-in-law Ralph Bondon called him to fill in one night. DiCapo was employed with the IRS, but after that night, he never went back to it. He fell in love with the restaurant business, because working with people was more interesting to him than accounting.

DiCapo's mother, Caroline "Kelly" Bivona DiCapo, and Virginia DiCapo Markese ran the kitchen along with other Italian women after Teresa passed away in 1947. They made marinara sauce, soup, ravioli, meatballs, lasagna,

IL TROVATORE

ITALIAN RESTAURANTS

No. 1—Independence Ave. and Locust.   No. 2—N. E. Corner 13th and Walnut, Second Floor.

OPEN
ALL
DAY

"FAMOUS
for Our
TASTY FOODS"

Thanksgiving Table d'Hote
Dinner **$1.25**

Antipasti
Chicken Noodle Soup
Spaghetti
Roast Turkey, with Cranberry Sauce
and Italian Chestnut Dressing
Combination Salad
Cauliflower in Butter
Mashed Potatoes
Home-made Pie or Ice Cream
Coffee or Tea

Genuine Italian Spaghetti and Ravioli

An early advertisement for Il Trovatore from the *Kansas City Star* (November 28, 1928). *From www.newspapers.com.*

pizza dough, cheesecake and cannoli. Before service, they passed the dishes "on to the men, who would add their own touch" of flavor and personality, recalled DiCapo. For traditional Italian-American cooking, "the comfortable form's peerless practitioner is Italian Gardens," decided *Kansas City Star* restaurant critic Art Siemering.[253]

"Investing in all that real estate on Baltimore Avenue was the best business decision my uncles ever made," wrote Carl J. DiCapo. "It was Baltimore—not Grand or Main—that was the real avenue of influence in Kansas City."[254] The frenetic energy of Hotel Row ensured the restaurant's booming business. In 1955, when Wachter Buffet closed at 1112 Baltimore Avenue, Italian Gardens took over the space and doubled its size (see chapter 9). Everyone mingled on Baltimore Avenue, many making their way to Italian Gardens for lunch or dinner, conviviality and conversation. The staff treated patrons as "guests" long before the term became established in the catering industry. Truckers, ex-cons, nightclub singers, theatrical troupes, families in from the suburbs, welterweight boxers, workers coming off their shifts, prom dates and Gray Line tourists patronized Italian Gardens when downtown was the nation's crossroads.

Italian Gardens became a victim of cultural shifts and infrastructure decisions beyond its control—most notably the significant downsizing of Municipal Downtown Airport after KCI opened. Department store closings, the riddling of a cohesive city center with interstate highways, urban blight and suburban flight meant that even the most established restaurants suffered. DiCapo retired in 1999. "Dad worked eighty hours a week," wrote his son Carl Michael. "He wore all the dark walnut stain off the wall behind his spot near the front door where he would lean back on his hands."[255] Frank Lipari died that same year at the age of ninety-three. Another longtime owner, Carolyn DiCapo-Bondon-Berbiglia, became ill. When the restaurant closed in December 2003, DiCapo recalled it as a sad day, but sadder still was that his restaurant was torn down to put up what downtown had become famous for: another parking lot. "I cried like a baby and could probably have died at that point," DiCapo wrote. "I'd spent forty-six years of my life there. I was there when I was single. I was

Italian Gardens right before it was razed. *Courtesy of Missouri Valley Special Collections, Kansas City Public Library (Kansas City, MO).*

there when I got married. I was there when I had my three sons. I spent my entire life there....But anyway, that's life. Nothing lasts forever."[256]

While Italian Gardens did not last, Carl DiCapo's son John David DiCapo has kept the legacy alive with his Italian Gardens Pizzeria, which sells the classics of the old restaurant, including Italian beef and steak sandwiches, pizza and Italian cookies. By using the products of local companies, such as Scimeca's sausage and Roma's bread and rolls, John DiCapo is likewise committed to preserving a wider Italian culinary heritage, one that informs Kansas City's distinctive foodways.

Ross' Il Pagliaccio

Another early Italian restaurant was the Ross family's Il Pagliaccio. Mamie (also Mayme) Pasano Ross and her husband, Joseph G. Ross, did not start out cooking for a profit, but to satisfy their own hunger and the hunger of those who stopped by their dressmaking and dry goods shop at Sixth and Cherry Streets, increasingly for meals as well as for business. Mamie, a first-generation Sicilian, oversaw the meals. Her homemade pasta garnered so many compliments that the couple converted a back room of their shop into a restaurant.[257]

The fluidity of movement, from dressmaking to cooking, makes it difficult to date the opening of Ross' Il Pagliaccio to a specific year; however, mentions of it appear in newspapers from 1928 (family-run advertisements date it to 1920). By the 1930s, the restaurant had expanded to seat around one hundred guests who could choose to sit in booths with pull drapes for privacy or at central aisle tables.

Mamie oversaw the kitchen, and Joseph oversaw the front of the house. Il Pagliaccio specialized in homemade spaghetti topped with rich tomato gravy and large meatballs, the size of which exemplified not only the availability of meat in Kansas City but also the newfound prosperity of so many Italian Americans. Tortellini and ravioli were also popular, topped with mushroom and Italian sausage sauce. WHB's *Swing* praised the restaurant's homey Italian dinners, the "glittery bar at one end of the room" and the sweet little figure of Il Pagliaccio gracing a wall niche. Patrons came also for the music, with Dave McClain giving "a mighty fine grand of piano music."[258]

Mamie and Joseph's son Frank Joseph Ross Sr. grew up in the restaurant. This former all-American fullback on the University of Missouri's football team was a gregarious, generous man who took over the business with his wife, Fanny, in 1948 after returning from World War II. Fanny ran the kitchen, and Frank worked the front of the house. Mamie stayed on as a

A postcard depicting Il Pagliaccio. *Courtesy of Missouri Valley Special Collections, Kansas City Public Library (Kansas City, MO).*

manager. The restaurant did not change its character but further cemented itself as "an intimate place which doesn't force you to rob a bank or take a mortgage on your home in order to afford your fare," as Frank characterized the restaurant in newspaper advertisements. Patrons enthusiastically agreed with Frank's description.

In 1953–54, Il Pagliaccio moved to 229 West Seventy-Fifth Street due to the construction of the Sixth Street Expressway. Shortly thereafter, Frank sold that location to Dan Mancuso, who operated it as Mancuso's Il Pagliaccio before changing its name to Mancuso's Gondola Restaurant. Various other shorter-lived branches of Ross' Il Pagliaccio operated at 609 West Forty-Eighth Street on the Country Club Plaza in the mid-1930s and, more significantly, at 804 Grand Boulevard in what had been the Federal Buffet, across from the federal courthouse. As a result, it became "an informal club for judges, newsmen, politicians, and businessmen," all of whom loved the food as much as Frank's personality, wrote Jean Haley.[259]

The final location of Ross' Il Pagliaccio opened in 1957 at East Fourth and Cherry Streets, close to the restaurant's original location. It had an "unconsciously continental atmosphere," made so by "the regular customers who congregate at the bar, the informal attitude of the staff, the bread sticks on the tables, and the lank busboy in the long white apron," wrote Dick Brown. It was a *Lady and the Tramp*–type of restaurant, with "red-and-white-striped tablecloths and candles in wine bottles….All that was missing were singing cooks," recalled Dan Costello.[260]

"There was just no experience like insulting and being insulted by Frank Ross," mourned Earl Stover after Frank's death in February 1972. Fanny felt it was best to close, and she sold the restaurant.[261] Nonetheless, Ross' Il Pagliaccio, Italian Gardens and LaSala established what, for decades, remained Kansas City's idea of a perfect Italian restaurant—models that newcomers often did well to imitate.

A MID-CENTURY LOVE AFFAIR WITH ITALIAN CUISINE: GAETANO'S AND MARIO'S

Critical to the story of simultaneously establishing traditions while also building on them is Jasper's and Cascone's, two of Kansas City's longest-surviving mid-twentieth-century Italian restaurants that continue to reap awards and maintain a robust patronage (see chapter 10). They and the other Italian restaurants that opened in the 1950s rode the crest of Italian cuisine's popularity in an era when Kansas Citians sought out Italian food rather than needing to be introduced to it. Two names stand out: Gaetano's, which opened in 1956 and became famous for its pizza, and Mario's, which opened in 1969 and became famous for its grinder. Both spanned a fascinating era in Kansas City's Italian restaurant history, an era that had concluded by the early 2000s, with many distinctive family-run affairs threatened by franchises and chains, particularly those that transformed pizzas and grinders into mere convenience foods—or worse, cheap junk food.

Gaetano's

Gaetano's was opened at 400 East Fifth Street when Mr. and Mrs. Charles Sciandrone sold their Venice Café (a tavern) to Edward J. Bruni and Thomas Passantino in 1955. The name Gaetano referenced the fact that Italians named Gaetano were often renamed Thomas.[262] The owners added a striking redwood front, installed a modern kitchen and redecorated the interior. Patrons loved the southern Italian–American pasta specials, but pizza was on the rise in popularity, and people were eager to try it; Dick Brown's September 1956 *Kansas City Star* column likely made people even more eager.

Brown divided Kansas City–style pizza into two categories. LaBruzzo's Tavern at 1809 Grand, a favorite hidey hole for journalists, excelled in "thin, rather crisp crust." Meanwhile, Gaetano's excelled in crust that "concentrates more on flavor and richness…than on thinness." Gaetano's pizza came out "heaping with whatever goodies are specified—I'm a mushroom man, myself," Brown admitted. It was also about high-quality ingredients, including liberal chunks of pepperoni and homemade Italian sausage.[263] Gaetano's signature sauce likewise had zing, and in that era, anchovies were a given, unless customers requested that they be left off.

The downtown area's redevelopment promised endless headaches, and meanwhile, Gaetano's outgrew its building.[264] The owners relocated in 1969 to the downtown high-rise River Hills Mark I in the River Hills Apartment Complex, a "city within a city," at 600 East Eighth Street. What had been a rather casual Italian restaurant became, at its second location, one of Kansas City's "smart" restaurants. The Clarendons, in their *Restaurant Guide to Greater Kansas City*, praised its "outstanding Italian decor," and certainly, the restaurant's sophistication complemented the modern urban architecture that then surrounded it.[265] Guests entered via a lobby that displayed the

Left: The front cover of the original Gaetano's menu. *Courtesy of Santamary Lozano.*

Right: An excerpt of Gaetano's menu from its second location. *Courtesy of Santamary Lozano.*

Gaetano Coat of Arms. The main dining area, the Pedagogue Room, featured a fireplace with a painting of Venice above the mantle. Black upholstered chairs and booths were graced with hand-carved dividers to offer privacy. Shades of mottled avocado and black worked well with marble wall inserts and cork paneling. A smaller dining area, the St. Thomas More Room, was perfect for parties. Windows overlooking the downtown airport runway added dramatic effect.[266]

Gaetano's pizza, by this time, was well known, with *Kansas City Star* restaurant reviewers Jess Ritter and Jane P. Fowler praising it. "There are those who go to Gaetano's…and select a filet or a top sirloin rather than the best pizza in town," Fowler wrote resignedly. How, she wondered, could they resist that "flaky delicate crust generously heaped with a virtual delicatessen of delights?"[267] The restaurant's other specialties included pasta topped with white clam sauce. The Clarendons singled out pasta Florentine.[268]

Gaetano's relied on River Hills residents and those from the nearby Vista del Rio Retirement Apartment Complex as regular patrons; they also relied on Southwestern Bell employees. It was also popular with TWA personnel and athletes who made Gaetano's a part of their visits to Kansas City. Joe Horlen of the Chicago White Sox singled it out as one of his three favorite Kansas City restaurants.[269]

From the late 1970s to the mid-1980s, Gaetano's withstood all manner of potential disruption—from the River Quay bombings to the onset of urban blight. However, it struggled to recover from a devastating 1984 fire. Although Bruni wanted to rebuild, complications with the lease stymied his ability to do so. In February 1986, Gaetano's returned to operation but as a carry-out pizzeria, confined to what had been the restaurant's storage area. Patrons drove into the Mark I parking garage to pick up orders.

The fire occurred during an invasion of pizza chains specializing in home delivery. Gaetano's had little choice but to join the competition, although Bruni tried to hold out. "Domino's created the monster of delivery," he said, "and this tells me delivery is something we have to do just to be competitive."[270] Delivering pizza downtown, with its congested streets, difficult parking and elevator waits, cost Gaetano's money when profit margins were already thin. To stay afloat financially, Bruni expanded his pizza business, maintaining his downtown operation while opening a location at 9918 West Eighty-Seventh Street in Overland Park, where parking was easy and delivery was straightforward. He also franchised his brand, with Jay Saner opening a Gaetano's at 11030 Quivira Road in 1987. In the early 1990s, Gaetano's popped up throughout the metro area, including in Kansas City's Northland and Independence, Missouri.

The fact that the Gaetano's name still carried such weight in the early 1990s testified to the cravings that generations of Kansas Citians carried with them for Gaetano's pizza. When Edward Bruni passed away in 1997, so did Gaetano's—although we are lucky that one of Bruni's acolytes was a young Gary Wilson. Working to learn Bruni's techniques, Wilson so impressed the pizza maestro that he gave his pizza recipes to Wilson. Today, Wilson's Pizza and Grill at 1801 Quindaro Boulevard in Kansas City, Kansas, turns out extraordinary pies that meet Bruni's daughter's— as well as this author's—approval.

Mario's

"A new Italian food specialty, which has brought its enterprising Kansas City inventor a certain local fame, is soon to be registered with the U.S. Patent Office and about to receive national publicity," announced Jane P. Fowler in

1971.[271] She was calling attention to Mario Scaglia and his brother Joe, who opened Mario's Delicatessen at 204 Westport Road the year Gaetano's had moved to larger quarters. Indeed, Mario Scaglia's grinder, his version of the Italian hero sandwich, put a national spotlight on Kansas City's gastronomy when *New York Times* food critic Mimi Sheraton spread its fame.

The Scaglias wanted "something more than just meatballs between Italian bread that was split open," Mario explained. Grinders, whose roots lay in Connecticut and who were still largely localized to New England, referred to a sandwich so thick and huge that it produced a lot of grinding, "wear-and-tear on a man's jaw bones," as a Hartford, Connecticut journalist put it.[272] The brothers took the name in a different, albeit just as literal, direction. Sheraton described the brothers' process: Mario's starts with "an individual-size loaf of Italian bread, roughly eight inches long. One end is sliced off about two inches from the top and set aside." Using a drill, the cooks "grind out" the loaf to "about a one-inch lining," into which they stuff three or four medium-size cooked and cubed meatballs or two or three cooked and sliced Italian sausages." Next come mozzarella or provolone cubes, followed by "half a cup of hot oregano and tomato pizzaiola sauce, in which the meatballs or the sausages were cooked."[273] To keep the sandwich's innards from spilling out, the cooks ingeniously shoved the bread plug back into the hole, foil-wrapped the grinder and baked it. Quickly, lines formed outside Mario's door.

By 1976, the Scaglias had sold their Westport Mario's to Robert L. Waid Sr., the head of the eponymous family restaurant chain. It continued to sell the grinder along with other Italian deli staples. Meanwhile, Mario and his wife, Kathy, and Joe and his wife, Rebecca, opened a fashionable Italian restaurant on the Plaza at 4747 Wyandotte Street, and they specialized in dishes topped with "Mom" Josephine Scaglia's sauce, the recipe that came with the family from Italy. Mario's also offered an array of dishes that were just coming into popularity in Kansas City that decade, including Mario Scaglia's interpretation of fettucine Alfredo, where noodles napped in butter and cream were served with chicken breast. The grinder was a lunchtime fixture.

As with many Plaza restaurants, Mario's was devastated by the September 1977 flood that put the Plaza under five feet of water. In its recovery, the restaurant shed what Shifra Stein called its "stuffy" elegance. "In a way, the flood was good for us," Joe Scaglia agreed. "It forced us to get back to the basics of a warm Italian family restaurant, which we started out with ten years ago."[274] Mario's eliminated the formal dress code, and patrons then entered a more intimate dining room, with "brick arches, wrought iron, and Tiffany lamps," wrote the Clarendons. "Immediately upon entry," one could wait for a table at the large bar "surmounted by a colorful, stained-glass ceiling." It was hugely popular. Former hostess Allison Smith recalled that in the early 1980s, "even with reservations, on weekends, people often waited an hour for their table."[275]

The Scaglias moved in 1991 to 4801 Jefferson Street and renamed their restaurant Caffe Mario to offer the even more relaxed vibe that many diners wanted. A small space, Caffe Mario no longer accepted reservations, and its all-day menu featured sandwiches (including the ever-popular grinder), salads and appetizers, such as the still-novel fried mozzarella cheese. Meals began with Italian bread and olive oil instead of older-fashioned whipped butter. John Martellaro praised the angel hair pasta in a "mellow, nutty cream sauce with fresh spinach."[276]

By the twenty-first century, the Scaglias were one of the city's most prominent restaurant families, with Mario's eateries scattered throughout the metro area. Mario and Kathy helped their daughters Jo Marie and Kathy A. Scaglia Green set up their own restaurants while they moved into retirement. John Waid, who had taken over the Westport Mario's, was likewise ready to sell his business in 2017, and although longtime employee Shelia Shields continued to make the famous grinders at the same Westport location (changed to Shelia's Grinder Shop), disputes with the landlord led to its closing. Meanwhile, as with pizza, the grinder became largely associated with national chains as a fast-food meal—not something to be gushed over in the *New York Times* for the care with which it was made or the distinctiveness of one family's innovation.

MOVING TOWARD THE FUTURE: VICTOR FONTANA'S FANNY'S RESTAURANT AND DISCOTHEQUE

Victor J. Fontana's Fanny's shows the evolution of Italian cuisine from the early twentieth century to the 1970s, when it opened. Fanny's broke implicit rules about what *Italian* meant to Kansas Citians and how and where the cuisine should be consumed—but it did so with style and grace. "We thought there were people, maybe older people, who would like to be around [a disco] kind of atmosphere but not dance themselves. And they love it, they do," Fontana told Jane P. Fowler shortly after Franny's opened. "They're asking to sit by the windows to observe the dancers below," he continued.[277] If it's a bit hard to visualize, it was because Fanny's Restaurant & Discotheque was unique. Its impact on Kansas City's dining scene was unprecedented, capturing the midtown zeitgeist of the 1970s and '80s. From its opening in April 1976, the place throbbed with excitement.

Fontana carried on in his parents' footsteps, building off what they taught him about hospitality and food. For forty-eight years, Fontana's father and mother had operated Frank's Place at Eighteenth and Cherry Streets. Regulars loved Katie Fontana's lasagna, spaghetti and meatballs, and as Fontana explained, his "dad knew the people who were his customers.…He was the best bartender in town because he was the best 'people' man." After he graduated from Rockhurst College, Fontana "was completely bewildered about what to do," so when his uncle became ill, Fontana's mother suggested that he help his dad for a couple of days. "Those couple of days turned into eleven years," Fontana told Fowler.[278]

Fontana first opened Walter Mitty's Nightclub in 1972. He worked the tables as his father had done, treating patrons like they were "somebodies," remarked Charles Ferruzza.[279] Walter Mitty's success led Fontana to move temporarily to Clayton, outside of St. Louis, to open another branch there. However, Fontana could not help but note and be inspired by St. Louis's Italian restaurant heritage, particularly Rich & Charlie's and Tony's. Also integral to Fontana's story were Chef Steve Neulle, maître d'hôtel Jimmy Valli and table captain Sam Garozzo. The three men moved to Kansas City to help Fontana create Fanny's. Valli composed the menu, pulling together his and Neulle's recipes. "We wanted to bring these—and some new ideas in a restaurant—to Kansas City," Valli told Fowler.[280]

With financing from realtor David L. Simpson II, who owned a warehouse at 3954 Central Street, Fontana transformed the square building, installing a disco on the ground floor and a second-story restaurant with sound-proof glass walls above that allowed diners to gaze down on the action. With disco being all the rage in Kansas City, a location off Westport and a menu featuring high-end specialties, Fanny's was immediately popular, driving patrons toward its "white cloth" formality instead of away from it. The novelty of a disco helped, but so did the restaurant's exclusiveness. Shifra Stein described Fanny's as "very 'New York.' It is chic and low-keyed and loaded with intimate atmosphere."[281] Fanny's disrupted fine-dining stiff properness while nonetheless keeping with the protocols, and patrons could not get enough of it.

While Italian Gardens and Gaetano's offered many main courses that did not involve either pasta or red sauce, those familiar staples were still prominent on their menus. Fanny's, along with Jasper's, instead highlighted dishes that situated Italy not as an entity isolated from Europe but rather as a part of the continent that shared culinary traditions with France, in particular. Fanny's excelled at Dover sole in lemon butter sauce, roasted duck in a champagne fruit sauce and veal with artichoke hearts. Fanny's also introduced diners to orecchiette and combinations such as pasta in cauliflower and cream, thus expanding diners' understanding of what *Italian* meant. Fanny's northern-influenced preparations were not as well known, explained Lazer Avery, who became chef when Steve Neulle moved on.[282]

Fontana also took inspiration from St. Louis, especially his scampi alla Giordano, the "most unusual version of scampi I've ever eaten," Stein wrote. Named after one of Fontana's relatives, the dish brought much fame to Fanny's. "Instead of shrimp, it was actually African lobster tail, lightly tossed in seasoned breadcrumbs, skewered, and charcoal broiled and topped with lemon and butter…So delicious it brought tears of joy to my eyes, it was rich, yet light," Stein enthused. Avery agreed: "It's a dish that is greater than the sum of its parts." Combine the parts, cook them just right and it is "exquisite."[283]

Served at Garozzo's Ristorante as "Shrimp Spiedini Maggie," Fontana's creation used African lobster tail and was perhaps the precursor to Garozzo's delicious entre. *Author's photograph.*

If the method for the dish sounds familiar to Kansas City and St. Louis readers, it is. One of Fontana's workers was Mike Garozzo, Sam Garozzo's cousin, who was also from St. Louis. The family made beef *spiedini*, Italian for "skewers"; they breaded, skewered and grilled beef chunks. When Mike Garozzo opened his eponymous restaurant in Columbus Park in 1989, he was, as was Sam Garozzo, familiar with the technique, one that was unusual if not entirely unknown in Kansas City Italian restaurants of that era. However, rather than using beef or chicken (what Mike did after his Uncle Alfio suggested the idea), Fontana wanted to "kick it up a notch," explained Avery, "using expensive seafood for his interpretation."[284] Its price at the time, Avery noted, was $10.50, comparable in 1976 to the highest-priced main course on the American Restaurant menu: Maine lobster Newburg that likewise sold for $10.50.[285]

Tragically, a fire consumed Fanny's in February 1978, but Fontana nonetheless rebuilt Fanny's from the ground up, maintaining most of the same features and layout as the original but adding a second-floor lounge. Again, the restaurant achieved status, but behind the scenes, it was suffering financially, and in 1985, it closed. By 1986, it had become Fontana's Chequer's Nightclub & Café, a more casual concept. Fontana maintained a strong presence in hospitality circles and was one of the city's most important restaurateurs. When he passed away in 2012, culinarians mourned and remembered him for often helping them get their own start, working at one of Fontana's many establishments. While Fanny's was short-lived, its impact continues to reverberate, having made other styles of Italian food not only popular in Kansas City but, by this point, expected.

9
Other Immigrant Influences

Kansas City's food heritage is enriched by continuous waves of immigration, beginning when French explorers encountered the Osage and Kansa in the vicinity of Kawsmouth in the 1700s. The following restaurants were owned by immigrants who made a significant contribution to Kansas City's status for great food and hospitality.

GERMAN LOST RESTAURANTS

Without the steady flow of German immigrants into Kansas City throughout much of the nineteenth and early twentieth centuries, Kansas City's culinary heritage would be markedly diminished.[286] Not only is the German brewing industry integral to that heritage but so are a host of food specialties, chief among them sausages, bread, cakes and classic German fare, such as sauerbraten. By the late twentieth century, many German specialties simply became part of an American mainstream diet not identified as "German," especially lager beer, pretzels, hotdogs and hamburgers. The first part of this chapter traces that evolution.

WACHTER'S BUFFET-LUNCH

Frank X. Wachter, a Hohenzollern emigrant, began as a saloonkeeper at Eleven East Twelfth Street in 1895. By 1927, Wachter and his wife,

Ernestine, were operating a buffet-lunch at Seventeen West Twelfth Street. Better remembered was Wachter's Buffet at 1112 Baltimore Avenue, which opened in 1934. Wachter's specialized in salads, pickled herring, cheeses and sausages and especially sandwiches, including German favorites such as liverwurst, pork roast and roast beef piled on rye bread and served with spicy-hot mustard accompanied by lager.[287]

Frank Wachter passed away in 1940, but his family continued to operate three eateries after his death, including the 1112 Baltimore Avenue location that lasted until 1955, when Italian Gardens took over the space (see chapter 8). The 105–7 East Twelfth Street location did not close until December 1970. Wachter's represented a time in Kansas City when German food was highly appreciated because it fulfilled many people's definition of a "square meal," particularly when sliced roast pork, sausages, kraut and potato salad were involved.

Meierhoff's German Restaurant

While Wachter's was associated with downtown, Erwin F. Meierhoff opened his restaurant on Kansas City's southside in 1959 on Sixty-Third Street, west of Troost Avenue. Erwin and his wife, JoAnn McLaughlin, wanted to own a restaurant that featured the foods of Erwin's heritage, and for years, Meierhoff's was synonymous with German cuisine.

Like Wachter's, Meierhoff's was highly regarded for its sandwiches, which it served in the basement rathskeller. Most came on pumpernickel with a side of sauerkraut or potato salad. Among the sausage selections were jagerwurst, knackwurst and bratwurst, which were popular at lunchtime. The dinner menu featured chicken paprikash, Wiener schnitzel, braised pigs' knuckles and sauerbraten, accompanied by red cabbage, potatoes and sauerkraut. Meierhoff's also offered an impressive number of imported German beers for that time. Society columnist Landon Laird loved the Munich dark beer on tap, in his opinion, the best he had ever downed.[288] For twenty-five years, Chef Betty J. Maxwell oversaw the cooking and was lauded for her potato pancakes with their distinctive onion flavor (she even offered cooking demonstrations), her rouladen smothered in a rich beef gravy and her sauerbraten.

Meierhoff's interiors benefited from JoAnn's expertise in repurposing antiques from historic razed properties. She traveled with a crowbar and a saw in her car trunk, on the lookout for treasures to incorporate in the restaurant. Indeed, Meierhoff's bar was a work of art, an antique Brunswick that she discovered in a Westport-Roanoke garage. "In fact," a reporter quipped, "the bar projected well beyond the garage....But it now occupies a rathskeller wall, floor-to-ceiling."[289]

From 1975 until it closed in 1993, Meierhoff's resided at 3800 Broadway Boulevard, and while it retained elements of its German menu, it became more associated with American mainstays, such as eggs Benedict and BLTs, as well as an atmosphere that combined conviviality with intellectual intensity. The city's powerbrokers held court every Saturday, starting with the 8:00 a.m. Serviss Group, described by Jeffrey Spivak as "ten hard-core" Democrats who met in a "room so dimly lit that it was hard to discern the color of the carpet." They weighed in on who had the best chances of a nomination for the next U.S. Senate race and city council elections, among other matters. Serviss left by 9:30 a.m. to make way for the next group of Democratic leaders. "It looks like a political hangout; the wooden tables and chairs give it the flavor of a Washington groupie's spot," said then-mayor Emanuel Cleaver, a frequent participant in these strategy sessions.[290]

When Meierhoff's was sold to Curtis Massood and Joe Guminger in 1993, it had become a ghost of its former self. The new owners kept Meierhoff's name but planned to modernize the interiors and create a new menu. Sadly, in February 1993, a fire destroyed the building. "We don't know what we'll do," Guminger told reporter Cynthia Lozano. "We're just glad to get out."[291] With costs so high and risks great, the owners sold the plot, and Meierhoff's became a memory.

BERLINER BEAR

By the time Meierhoff's closed, Berliner Bear at 7815 Wornall was Kansas City's most popular German restaurant. Karl J. Lindig fled Wittenberg, Germany, when its Soviet occupation after World War II put him in danger as a resistor. He made his way to Berlin, and from there, he came to the United States, first settling in Wichita, where his uncle lived. His father, Friedrich "Fritz," a former delicatessen owner, joined his son in 1962, and they wished to open a restaurant that reminded them of home. Because Berlin had been Karl's sanctuary from the Soviets, the men called the restaurant Berliner Bear.[292]

Although the building was nondescript, with one long rectangular dining room and a smaller side room, columnist Dick Brown praised the friendly service, sausages, sauerbraten, schnitzel and sauerkraut. It was also one of Kansas City's few places that served decent food after Starlight Theater's performances ended at 11:00 p.m.[293]

Karl's death in March 1973 threw the restaurant into uncertainty. What held it together were waitress Nettie Womack, also a German native, and her husband, Joel, one of the cooks. When Fritz and his wife returned to Germany, Joel became the general manager and Nettie became the assistant manager; in the 1980s, they likely assumed ownership. Nettie and Joel added jägerschnitzel and cordon bleu to the menu, along with a seasonal hasenpfeffer and roast goose dinner, which was popular during the holiday season.

Berliner Bear struggled as other German restaurants closed and Kansas Citians sought lighter, more novel cuisines. With Joel's passing in 1995, his son Bill took the helm of the restaurant along with Nettie. Her ailing health nonetheless took its toll on the restaurant's reputation. The rental of a back room to a neo-Nazi organization for a banquet brought "just enough local publicity to seriously sour the restaurant's already faltering business," wrote Charles Ferruzza on the restaurant's closing two years later.[294]

Most remember Berliner Bear at the height of its fame, however—the place where they first fell in love with German food. "I very fondly remember the Berliner Bear!" wrote Jayne Eggerstedt Johnson, an alum, along with the author, of North Kansas City High School's German Club. "It was stepping into Germany, right off Wornall. We would speak German, and the atmosphere was always festive."[295] Heaping plates of rouladen with red cabbage were popular, as were the one-of-a-kind potato dumplings. Almost to the end, Nettie handcrafted the apple strudel and baked Black Forest cherry cake, the most popular way to wrap up an evening of fine food and fun.

EASTERN EUROPEAN AND JEWISH LOST RESTAURANTS

Along with Germans seeking a new life in Kansas City were eastern Europeans, many of them Jewish. Their culinary traditions resembled those of the Germans, particularly those who emigrated from Poland, Austria and Hungary. Specializing in pastry, deli items and noodle and meat dishes, these restaurateurs made lasting marks on the city's wider culinary tastes and are still remembered today.

New York Bakery and Delicatessen

Esther and Isadore Becker's New York Bakery and Delicatessen stayed in business for almost a century and was mourned when it closed in 2009. Over its lifespan, it was owned by two different families, and its patron base went from being roughly 90 percent Jewish to roughly 60 percent Black. During these demographic transitions, the owners adapted and, in the process, created a distinctive Jewish delicatessen tradition that brought national attention.

Isadore Becker and Esther Lessner Becker came from baking backgrounds in Poland. After settling in Kansas City, Esther's brother Jacob started the Lessner Bakery. He organized the Jewish Specialty Bakers of Kansas City in 1936. Isadore worked as a baker in 1908 for Samuel I. Eisberg and in 1914 for Henry Shefrin. After saving money, Isadore and Esther bought a building permit for a brick oven with a stone base for their own bakery, and based on that date, they likely began their business in 1917 at 919 East Eighteenth Street.[296]

The Beckers specialized in crusty ryes and pumpernickels, challahs for Shabbat, many bagel varieties and kosher delicatessen staples. The quality and uniqueness of their goods raised their profile, and many people began patronizing the establishment. In 1920, the business moved to 1721 East Thirty-First Street, but most people remember its final location at 7016 Troost Avenue. In 1951, a branch of Eybel Bakeries at that location went bankrupt, and the Beckers bought the equipment and building. In the 1950s, Troost Avenue was a busy commercial corridor for everything from car dealerships to restaurants. Jewish neighborhoods clustered between Holmes and Troost Avenue, and traffic was steady. For a short time, the Beckers also operated a location at Thirty-Ninth and Troost Avenue near a busy bus stop.

In 1957, the Beckers retired to Florida and left the business to their son Manuel and his wife. For the next twenty-plus years, the business remained largely unchanged, famous for its hot pastrami on rye, kosher frankfurters, salty lox and marinated herring. A new generation of customers treated the delicatessen and owners like a second home and family.

In 1980, after his wife's death, Manuel retired and sold the business to James and Barbara Holzmark. The neighborhoods were still, according to James's interview with historian David Sax, 90 percent Jewish at that time, and the establishment remained an anchor for families who relied on it for their bagels and the city's best gefilte fish and matzo cakes for Passover.[297]

Kansas City's growing love affair with bagels also aided business. During the 1980s and 1990s, low-fat diets became the craze, and people searched for an alternative to donuts. The Holzmarks offered more than a dozen bagel flavors, along with lebkuchen cookies, schnecken, pumpernickels and ryes. Charles Ferruzza singled out the challah: "It's great for sandwiches, and…it makes the very best French toast."[298] The Holzmarks also expanded to include a seating area (prior, it was take-out only), and they introduced its signature, much-missed Reuben. With the name New York Delicatessen, the Holzmarks wanted a sandwich that evoked New York City. "You can't get more New York than a Reuben," James explained to Matthew Schofield.[299] The corned beef arrived from Chicago in barrels of brine, was sliced, piled onto bread, layered with house-made kraut and slathered with spicy brown mustard and mayonnaise instead of thousand island dressing. Many patrons considered it Kansas City's finest sandwich and said it was worth a detour.

When Temple B'nai Jehudah moved to Overland Park to follow the many Jewish residents who were leaving for the suburbs, the line at the counter of New York Bakery and Delicatessen became increasingly occupied by Black people. The Holzmarks responded with a new masterpiece: kosher smoked brisket, the brainchild of longtime head baker and brisket maker Sonny Taborn. He rubbed brisket with a secret spice blend and smoked it in a custom-built metal box for six hours with hickory. Sax bit into a portion, chewed and described it as "mild, crumbly, and definitely smoky, a subdued and wonderful contrast to the powerful kick of pastrami with far more wood flavor in each bite.…A true example of Black/Jewish fusion."[300]

The cost of selling artisan meats, salads and breads to increasingly indifferent consumers hurt New York Bakery and Delicatessen's bottom line, however. The 2000s saw not only franchise and grocery bagels flood the metro area, but it also saw the invasion of cheap sandwich chains. It's worth noting that, to the end, the Holzmarks held on to their convictions about what their establishment meant. "We're a Jewish *delicatessen*, not a sandwich shop," James corrected Sax when Sax called it a deli. It was with a delicatessen that the Holzmarks ended their career in 2009, taking with them Kansas City's last surviving kosher option for house-made herring and sour cream, knishes, gefilte fish, pastrami, smoked brisket, challah and bagels.

MRS. LENNET'S CAFE AND WEISS CAFÉ

Readers might recall that Harry Weiss was the last restaurateur of repute in the Coates House Hotel (see chapter 2). Prior to that, he operated a lively café at 1215 Baltimore Avenue, specializing in Jewish and continental food. Chances are that, by this point, however, few will remember restaurateur Reltz Lennet. While no known information exists on the connections between Lennet and Weiss, their names are intertwined in early Kansas City's Jewish restaurant history. As early as 1913, the 1215 Baltimore Avenue address itself was associated with Jewish restaurants, a culinary legacy that deserves closer investigation.

Reltz Jankelewna Lennet, née Biszkowicz, immigrated to the United States in the early 1900s, as did her brother, Izaak. They were Polish Jews whose earliest records in Kansas City place them in the culinary industry, although when Izaak died in 1964, he was known as a scholar and musician. Izaak risked deportation to Poland in 1936, but a judge ruled that he be allowed to remain in Kansas City, where he managed his sister's restaurant at 1215 Baltimore Avenue.[301]

Harry Weiss, born in Hungary, arrived in Kansas City around 1915, but he also spent time working with family in Hollywood, California, to open Café Vienna in 1930. Harry lived in Los Angeles on and off during the 1920s and 1930s but returned to Kansas City for good in 1939. As with Lennet and Biszkowicz, Weiss's name is associated with the same 1215 Baltimore Avenue address—sometimes concurrently, especially in 1925, 1939 and 1940.[302]

Another name also comes into play: a Mr. Singer, who operated his eponymous Hungarian-Jewish café at 1215 Baltimore Avenue in the 1910s. A December 22, 1913 Singer's Café want advertisement sought a woman who knew Jewish cooking and who was preferably Slavic- or German-speaking. Nothing is known about Mr. Singer, but it is possible that Weiss and/or Lennet were connected to this café during Singer's time. Mr. Singer's Café specialized in Hungarian noodles, goulash and roast poultry, dishes that both Weiss and Lennet would have known well.

By 1921, Singer's name had vanished from the culinary world. Lennet's did, too, when she retired in 1940. After 1949, it was strictly Weiss Café. WHB's *Swing* touted its "kosher-style cookery and the town's most varied menu. The food is rich, and there's lots of it....Whole families like it for Sunday dinner powwows." Meanwhile, Harry Weiss's son Martin was also making his way in hospitality. *Swing* praised him as "a genial host" at the Café Fiesta in the nearby Ambassador Hotel. "The décor is Latin American, but you'll find gefultafish [*sic*], borscht, and kerplock [*sic*] on the widely varied menu."[303]

Harry Weiss moved to the Coates House Hotel in 1945–46, when Max Bretton moved to the 1215 Baltimore Avenue address (see chapter 5). Following Weiss was his loyal kitchen staff, especially Chef James "Jimmy" Halfacre. The staff was the key, explained Weiss's grandson Phillip. They "followed him wherever he hung his hat and should be credited with those traditional dishes that they replicated faithfully."[304]

For the next sixteen years, Weiss continued in the restaurant business. In 1955, he briefly worked alongside his son at the Bellerive Hotel's Café Boulevard at 214 East Armour Boulevard before finishing his career at Twin Oaks Apartment Complex, 5050 Oak Street, where he bought Benish's Restaurant. At all these places, vestiges of the Singer's Café menu stayed on Weiss's menu, with Chef Halfacre's roast brisket and potato pancakes being huge favorites, along with roast capon and duckling. In 1962, Weiss retired, and in 1963, he passed away. With him died a rich heritage of continental-Jewish cuisine that left Kansas City a bit poorer than it had been before.

JENNIE'S CAFÉ

Starting in the late 1800s, many eastern Europeans settled in Kansas City, Kansas, often taking meatpacking jobs. By 1920, some four thousand immigrants had arrived, many settling in the Strawberry Hill Neighborhood. Among them were Croatians John and Jennie L. Bukovac. Jennie worked in meatpacking before the family was financially secure enough for her to be a housewife and raise the couple's children. When they were older, Jennie and John purchased a small café at 402 North Fifth Street in Kansas City, Kansas, named it Jennie's, lived upstairs, had boarders and ran the business below. The year was 1950.[305]

Initially, the wider Kansas City community knew little about Jennie's. This unassuming family-run establishment catered to a clientele nostalgic for the flavors of their former homelands. "Everybody knows everybody," recalled Joe and Ann Dercher, regulars who ate there on Friday nights. Many started their weekend at Jennie's and then concluded it with Mass up the hill at St. John the Baptist Catholic Church. The Bukovac family, including grown children, as well as grandchildren, helped in the restaurant, with Andy and their daughter, Helen Bukovac Cromwell, becoming co-owners with their mother after John passed away. Frank and Marianne Bukovac Jaksa, daughter of Jennie's oldest son, purchased it in 1990.[306]

Construction and an exit off Interstate 70 onto North Fifth Street put countless drivers in Jennie's path in 1980. It beckoned to the curious who parked and checked out the food therein. They discovered, along with *Kansas City Star* critic Nancy Ball, that the wood-paneled interior with a friendly, comfortable ambiance "belied its faded exterior."[307] Everything about the restaurant exuded family, from the white cupboards to the knickknacks. The interiors lent themselves, wrote reporter Paul Hohl, to the neighborhood coffee gatherings that patrons looked forward to, especially the homemade povitica, a nut-filled yeast bread, or apple strudel.[308]

Along with baked goods, Jennie's served Croatian staples, such as sarma, a ground-beef-and-rice log wrapped and simmered in cabbage leaves, and strukla, like a homemade egg noodle, rolled into a log, sliced, sautéed in a little butter and served with porcupine meatballs and gravy. Polish sausage and braised sauerkraut were also popular staples, but so, too, were classic American "blue-plate specials," from pork chops and mashed potatoes to hot beef sandwiches.

As is often the case with cherished restaurants, Jennie's owners and cooks grew old and retired, and great-grandchildren carved out career paths that took them far from the family business. Mariann Jaksa, along with her husband and children, decided in 2000 that it was time to move on to other opportunities, despite the sadness that they and the customers experienced. Jaksa hoped someone would buy the restaurant and continue the tradition. Adis Hot and his family, who had fled the Bosnian War, did indeed buy it in 2001. They used their own family recipes but kept Jennie's name. Sadly, the restaurant struggled and shortly thereafter closed for good. To date, no restaurant has offered the Croatian staples that four generations of Kansas Citians found at Jennie's.

CHINESE LOST RESTAURANTS: KING JOY LO AND HOUSE OF TOY

Asian immigration to Kansas City began prior to World War II, when men from Guangdong Province, China, often took work in laundries and Chinese apothecaries. While Japanese, Vietnamese, Korean, Thai and Indian immigration increased after World War II, the longest-lived and best-known Asian restaurants in Kansas City were Chinese, and two stand out.

King Joy Lo Co. Mandarin Restaurant

Many older Kansas Citians were introduced to Chinese American food at King Joy Lo. In the early 1900s, the Chinese Empire Reform Association raised money for its causes by creating restaurants targeted at Westerners. The first King Joy Lo, managed by Chin F. Foin, opened in Chicago. Foin's brother, Chin Man Lee, resided in Kansas City. Kansas City's King Joy Lo, opened in 1908, was likely the result of that family connection. It made Chinese American cuisine more familiar, and the restaurant became a favorite of people out for special occasions, theatergoers and police officers on late-night beats.[309] It initially resided at 1217 Grand Boulevard, above the Princess Theater, before moving to 1203 Grand Boulevard, above a drugstore.

To attract business, the restaurant published lengthy advertisements designed to familiarize would-be diners with dishes prepared in "true Mandarin style." King Joy Lo satisfied Kansas City's newfound craving for chow mein and chop suey, steamed rice, almond cookies and hot tea. Also popular were the restaurant's magnificent stir fries, including one with black and white mushrooms, bean sprouts, water chestnuts, chicken, shrimp, beef and abalone, all bound together in an oyster sauce slurry, as Pat Price remembered the dish in a 1999 retrospective. Curious gourmets, Price recalled, could request more unusual fare, including bird's nest soup.[310]

In 1929, King Joy Lo moved to its final address, Eight West Twelfth Street, taking up the second, third and fourth floor of the Pennock Building, with Liggett's Drugstore (then Parkview Drugs) below and Paramount Theater next door.

Opposite: A September 20, 1908 King Joy Lo advertisement promoting the healthfulness of Chinese food. *From www.newspapers.com.*

Above: Main Street, north from Twelfth Street, with King Joy Lo's sign visible on the corner (1948). *Courtesy of Missouri Valley Special Collections, Kansas City Public Library (Kansas City, MO).*

Behind floor-to-ceiling windows, diners looked out on an intersection lit up in neon at night and teaming with pedestrians, streetcars and automobiles during the day. "King Joy Lo may not have provided a window on the world, but it offered the best view of Kansas City's crossroads," Ian Drake remembered.[311]

By the late 1920s, King Joy Lo was run by family members of its original founders, the Young and Toy families. Bo Sing Young, who also owned Bo Sing's Chinese Restaurant on the Plaza (until his death in 1935), and Harry and Don Toy, were all well-known men in art and restaurant circles. They went great distances to break through the racial prejudice that Chinese citizens routinely encountered.

A fire at Liggett Drugstore caused damage to King Joy Lo in 1938, briefly bankrupting the business, but another fire, which started in the basement of the Parkview Drugs in December 1961, brought an end to the venerable restaurant. Instead of reopening, Harry Toy joined his cousin, Don, at House of Toy, which had opened at 602 West Forty-Eighth Street in 1956 and thus continued a grand family culinary saga.[312]

House of Toy

Several family members ran House of Toy during its nearly four-decades-long existence. While it continued King Joy Lo's tradition of serving Cantonese-style fare, its menu also reflected evolving tastes in Chinese food. The Clarendons, in their *Guide to Kansas City Restaurants*, reported that it "is heaven for aficionados of egg rolls. They have the best that we have found in Kansas City…served hot on warm plates with sweet and sour sauce and good, hot mustard." The wonton soup was likewise popular, along with the beef and peapods.[313]

As with other Plaza restaurants discussed in previous chapters, House of Toy was devastated by the September 1977 flood. It was the hardest-hit business due to a gas explosion that also occurred as water poured in. It took nine months to rebuild, but when it returned, it resumed its same unpretentious atmosphere. "Red vinyl booths and chairs" do not "upstage the Cantonese food," Jan Paschal wrote in 1979.[314] It did little to advertise but maintained a following of patrons who loved its friendliness and food. It made the Plaza still feel a bit like what it originally was, a place where people in surrounding neighborhoods relied on its convenience and amenities more than treating it as a fashion statement.

In what reporter Joyce Smith called the J.C. Nichols Company's game of "musical restaurants," Harry Toy was forced to vacate his space in January 1993 to offer it to La Mediterranee, whose owners were likewise forced to vacate their larger space at 4742 Pennsylvania Avenue to make way for a bar and grill concept (see chapter 5). Unwilling to move the House of Toy into Seville Square Food Court (what the Nichols Company suggested), Harry Toy cast about for a new restaurant home but did not settle on one.[315] The result? Kansas City lost what had been a continuous family lineage of Canton-inspired Chinese cuisine that began in the early twentieth century and endured almost to the end of the century.

10
Still with Us After All These Years

Kansas City is fortunate. Its citizens do not tire easily of their favorite restaurants, so for a metropolitan area of moderate size, it nonetheless supports an astonishing number of eateries that have survived over three-quarters of a century.

Because the Lost Restaurants Series is about just that, restaurants that are now gone, this chapter will inevitably strike readers as frustratingly short and scanty. Take comfort, however, in the fact that many long-lasting icons are not only still open but, despite the challenges of COVID-19, are doing remarkably well. The two Kansas Cities' longest-surviving restaurants share one essential characteristic: they offer today's diners a direct link to past tastes and favorite foods. In other words, essential items on their menus, be it a bowl of chili, a tenderloin or a plate of cheese ravioli in marinara sauce, rely on recipes and techniques that have been handed down, intact, for three and as many as five generations.

Please use this chapter as a guidebook. Cherish the history of each restaurant that follows, yes, but make a point to visit and seek out the flavors of yesteryear to understand something about how these flavors have often dictated what Kansas Citians crave and expect from restaurants today. Without long-surviving restaurants to remind us of what we love foodwise, we become even more susceptible to the power of homogenizing chains and franchises that threaten our flavor palate and the culinary eccentricities that make Kansas City, Missouri, and Kansas City, Kansas, distinctive from other cities.

OUR OLDEST SURVIVING RESTAURANTS (1919–1938)

Dixon's Famous Chili (Dixon's Chili Parlor), 1919

9105 EAST U.S. HIGHWAY 40
INDEPENDENCE, MO

Vergne Dixon started his career in 1919, initially selling chili from a pushcart in downtown Kansas City, Missouri. From there, he opened his first Dixon's Chili Parlor at Fifteenth and Olive Streets. After his death in 1964, the family franchised the restaurant, and Dixon's Chili Parlors dotted the metro area. Today, the last remaining Dixon's is located in Independence, Missouri, where it does brisk business; indeed, in 2021, it won Kansas City's *Pitch*'s "best of" category for chili. Unlike the soupy, tomato-based gravy we often associate with chili, Dixon's is simply steamed ground chuck, barely seasoned. Customers tailor the chili to their tastes from an array of condiments, most importantly, the house-mixed chili powder and the fiery, chili-infused vinegar that have remained on the tables since the beginning. Customers can also choose to top their chili with pink beans, make it "soupy" by ordering it with bean broth, "juicy" with natural meat juices or "dry" (plain). From there, one adds garnishes, with one caveat: ketchup was anathema to Vergne Dixon, and if he caught a customer sneaking it in, he fined them. Grudgingly,

The last Dixon's Chili Parlor, in Independence, Missouri. *Author's photograph.*

he began offering it for an additional nickel, so today, Dixon's charges a nominal fee for ketchup to pay homage to its founder. Dixon's most famous customer was Harry S. Truman, who was photographed in 1950 by *LIFE* magazine enjoying a plate of chili at the original location on Olive Street. His patronage convinced the business to change its name to Dixon's Famous Chili. Today, the business is carried on by Terri Totta-Smith, the daughter of Vergne Dixon's nephew Leonard Totta. Leonard's grandson Stephen Steffes is next in line.

Arthur Bryant's Barbeque, circa 1927

1727 BROOKLYN AVENUE
KANSAS CITY, MO

Dating Bryant's (as it is usually known) opening is a somewhat fruitless task. As chapter 4 details, the connection between Henry Perry and his apprentice, Charlie Bryant, means that, for some time, Charlie worked under Perry's supervision. Most sources agree that in 1927, Charlie started his own business at Fourteenth and Woodland Streets. There, he created a "formula...that spread his fame as a barbecue man far and wide," stated his *Kansas City Call* obituary.[316] In 1929, Charlie had moved to 1921 East Eighteenth Street (Eighteenth and Euclid Streets). In 1931, Perry suffered a debilitating stroke that left him in need of a partner, and by all accounts, Charlie was the man. After Perry passed away in 1940, he left his business to Charlie, who rebranded it Bryant's Barbecue or sometimes Charlie Bryant Barbecue.[317]

Critical to the story is Charlie's brother, Arthur, who arrived in Kansas City from east Texas in 1931. When Arthur bought his brother's business after Charlie retired in 1946, he did little more than tame his brother's fiery sauce, add French fries to his menu (boiled in lard) and, by 1958, move to 1727 Brooklyn Avenue.

Calvin Trillin explained in 1990 that Bryant's Barbecue's national reputation helped Kansas Citians "recognize the legitimacy of their hometown." It made them proud to champion "grease houses" (as Arthur described his restaurant), along with fried chicken joints and hamburger shacks, many of which are still with us and are highlighted in this chapter.[318] Burnt ends (the charred bits off the brisket's point section after the fat renders) are credited directly to the Bryant brothers by barbecue historians. They

Arthur Bryant inside his restaurant (1981). *Courtesy of Missouri Valley Special Collections, Kansas City Public Library (Kansas City, MO).*

were what Arthur would put out for free for customers to snack on while they waited in line. Today, what was once discarded is "one of the trendiest items in contemporary barbecue," wrote food historian Adrian Miller. Burnt ends, as much as Calvin Trillin, brought Bryant's worldwide fame.[319]

Tenderloin Grill, 1932

900 SOUTHWEST BOULEVARD
KANSAS CITY, MO

Southwest Boulevard is home to several very old restaurants, with Tenderloin Grill being the oldest. Its story takes us back to the day when the lunch wagons and push carts reigned supreme on downtown and neighborhood streets. John Zachary Koury came to Kansas City around 1906, having moved from Tripoli, Lebanon. He operated a wagon in the vicinity of 800 Southwest Boulevard, from which he sold hotdogs, pig ears and pig snoot sandwiches, among other specialties. A 1937 newspaper article on Koury's business, "A Paradise for Wimpy," detailed a rivalry between Koury and a former employee of his who set up a lunch cart across the street from Koury's. A bidding war between the two brought the cost of sandwiches down to as little as one cent for each—much to the delight of the neighborhood.[320]

Koury's success led him to establish the Tenderloin Grill, a tiny café that sat roughly ten people, shortly thereafter. He worked alongside his grandson James J. Nabhan until his death in 1966. Nabhan continued the traditions set by Koury, serving his pig snoots, pig ears, fried chicken and pork tenderloin sandwiches, always with the accompaniment of mustard, hot sauce and horseradish, relishes that went well with fatty offal and fried foods in general. He kept irregular hours, opening when he wished, closing when he was out of product.[321]

One of the Tenderloin Grill's favorite customers was a young man named Richard Herrera, who lived nearby. He loved the fried tenderloins, a love that only grew when Herrera joined the military. He wished when he returned in 1960 to open a sandwich shop and specialize in them, and he ended up purchasing Nabhan's shop in 1975.

Until October 2021, Maria Herrera Ruhl and her daughter Ashlee Herrera ran the Tenderloin Grill, keeping things much the same, including the pig snoot sandwich, which was prominently displayed on the menu alongside the tenderloin sandwich. However, the business was hit hard by COVID-19, and the Herrera family was ready to sell. They did so to an enthusiastic longtime restaurateur, Gregg Johnson, founder of Minsky's Pizza and the Minsky's Pizza Restaurant Group, along with Angel Hernandez and other Minsky's Pizza Restaurant Group investors. The new owners have promised the Herrera family that they will continue operations as they have been done for ninety years.

Stroud's (Oak Ridge Manor), 1933

5410 NORTHEAST OAK RIDGE DRIVE
KANSAS CITY, MO

While Sandy's Oak Ridge Manor (see chapter 3) remained in operation until the early 1980s, most Kansas Citians know that location today as Stroud's North, which was started when Jim Hogan and Mike and Dennis Donegan saved Kansas City's most famous fried chicken restaurant from extinction.

Helen Stroud's story takes us back to 1933, when she and her husband, Guy, operated a barbecue/fireworks stand at East Eighty-Fifth Street, just over the Kansas City border (at the time) so that they could sell liquor on Sundays.[322] Stroud's was a roadhouse, the antithesis of the genteel teahouses discussed in chapter 3. Helen's decision to fry chicken had to do with war rationing and the cost of food. She mastered the craft, in part, by ensuring

The fried chicken dinner at Stroud's remains timeless. *Author's photograph.*

The original Stroud's at 1015 East Eighty-Fifth Street prior to its razing (2009). *Courtesy of Missouri Valley Special Collections, Kansas City Public Library (Kansas City, MO).*

that the chickens were fresh. She dredged them in flour, salt and pepper and fried them in skillets until they developed a shattering golden crust. Over time, "Helen" became a tamer "Mrs. Stroud," a respectable widow. Families began flocking to her restaurant, where Chef David Bragg oversaw a well-run kitchen. Stroud's attracted nationwide attention and became a destination restaurant as well as a local favorite. When Helen retired in 1972–73, the restaurant briefly closed until the Donegans and Hogan contacted Helen and secured her permission to continue to use her name and her Stroud's recipes. They revived Stroud's, only to have the city close its original location to widen Eighty-Fifth Street.

Today, the Stroud's Northeast Oak Ridge Drive location continues the tradition, having never compromised the quality of its meat. It has also never gone over to instant mashed potatoes, and it still makes hundreds of baskets of its addictive cinnamon rolls a day. Kansas Citians should count themselves lucky to be able to take this caliber of a fried chicken dinner for granted.

Rosedale Bar-B-Q, 1934

600 SOUTHWEST BOULEVARD
KANSAS CITY, KS

A "barbecue tree," writes Adrian Miller, describes "the influence of a barbecuer who trains or mentors others to become highly regarded pitmasters and/or restaurateurs."[323] Given Kansas City's unwavering love of barbecue, former apprentices and their barbecue teachers often see one another as compatriots, not competitors. When a pitmaster dies, the former apprentices who continue the tradition are often burnished in the glow of nostalgia and earn the regard of customers who celebrate an uninterrupted tradition of smoking meat.

That's how it was with Henry Perry on the Missouri side and Anthony and Alda Rieke and Tony Sieleman on the Kansas side when they opened for business in 1934. Still operating on Southwest Boulevard, Rieke's granddaughter and Sieleman's great-niece Marisha Brown-Smith keeps the business humming along.

Anthony Rieke had to learn to barbecue "from scratch"; he was the trunk of a new barbecue tree. Anthony and Alda were farmers whose business was harmed by Depression-era drought and grasshoppers. To make up for lost

Rosedale Barbecue today, with its old stools still largely intact. *Author's photograph.*

income, they decided to grill hotdogs, because they were cheap and readily available. The business took off, but the aroma of hickory smoke from "Fatty" Sharp's nearby barbecue stand on Southwest Boulevard convinced Anthony and Sieleman to learn how to barbecue.[324]

"Grandpa Rieke had built numerous houses and was also mechanically inclined from growing up fixing farm equipment," Brown-Smith said. Knowing that the business would only grow if he could expand his smoking operations, Rieke "went home to his farm, drew out an idea, and constructed his version of a rotating rotisserie oven and smoke box," Brown-Smith continued. "To make sure it would operate correctly, he had his farm hands load Rieke [himself] onto one of the racks and rotated it." It worked—"like riding a carnival ride," recalled Brown-Smith. With the mechanism for smoking meat in place, the next obstacle was learning the art of barbecue. Rieke's "philosophy was if you burn it up once or twice, you'll learn pretty quick," Brown-Smith chuckled.

Without fanfare, Rosedale Barbecue quietly grew into a neighborhood and then a citywide institution, setting up a distinctive Kansas City, Kansas, legacy as the Riekes and Sieleman trained employees who set up their own businesses. Among them was Sieleman's nephew Earl Quick (see chapter 4), as well as the owners of Merriam BBQ, Johnny's Barbecue, Daniel's and Porky's Pit. Ronald E. Williams, who started Wyandotte Barbecue in the late 1970s (now with two locations: 8441 State Avenue in Kansas City, Kansas, and 7215 West Seventy-Fifth Street in Overland Park, Kansas), learned the art of barbecuing while managing Rosedale Barbecue.

While many newer barbecue restaurants have done away with barbecued ham, Rosedale keeps it on the menu, along with the humble foods that gave the Riekes and Sieleman their start, like the grilled hotdogs and chili dogs, as well as smoked flash-fried chicken, an essential protein to replace pork and beef during the worst days of the Depression and World War II. Rosedale Barbecue remains steadfast to its founders' traditions and thus offers a flavor that takes us back to the 1930s.

Town-Topic Hamburgers, 1937

2021 Broadway Boulevard and 1900 Baltimore Avenue
Kansas City, MO

Barbecue and steak often overshadow Kansas City's reputation for great hamburgers, but Thrillist routinely reminds us that hamburgers matter, especially Town-Topic's. As of 2021, Thrillist reaffirmed Town-Topic as "one of the finest renditions of a diner burger in America, 24/7, [in] downtown KC."[325]

A classic Town Topic combination: a cheeseburger and tater tots. *Author's photograph.*

Two Town-Topics remain; Thrillist referenced the 2021 Broadway Boulevard address, which dates to 1944, the year that founders Claude J. Sparks and Haywood Billing dissolved their partnership. Haywood kept the original Town-Topic the men had built in 1937 at 2442 Broadway Boulevard. Sparks took the remaining five. Along with the 2021 Broadway Boulevard address, diners can still indulge their hamburger cravings at the 1900 Baltimore Avenue address as well.

Iconic Restaurants of Kansas City

The hamburger is not the only menu item that literally takes diners back to 1937—so does the chili, described by Charles Ferruzza as a "highly seasoned, dark concoction with lots of ground beef."[326] During the Depression, diners could order a five-cent bowl of it with saltine crackers to take an edge off their hunger.

Today, Town-Topic Hamburgers is owned by the grandson of the founder, Scott Sparks. As with many owners of long-established restaurants in Kansas City, Sparks does what he can to keep his supply chain local, with his beef custom ground in nearby Independence by L&C Meat.[327] Other favorite menu items include the all-day breakfast, which is customized to each patron's wishes and is prepared by a cook a mere three feet or so from where the patron sits.

Dagwood's Café, 1938

1117 SOUTHWEST BOULEVARD
KANSAS CITY, KS

While we don't hear the term anymore, back in the early twentieth century, tiny cafés were often called *eat shops*. They served as kitchens for people with limited cooking space in their homes. While eat shops could seat a handful of patrons, most ordered their food to carry out. Kansas City's working-class neighborhoods were full of eat shops, for laborers who worked long hours with limited time to sleep and eat before their next shift began. Dagwood Eat Shop, as it was originally called, was named for the sandwich-loving character Dagwood from the *Blondie* comic strip.[328]

Information on the original owner is obscure. Its two most-remembered proprietors were James "Jimmie" Brown Coe and former waitress/manager Ruby Morlan. She bought the business in 1993, along with her husband, Dennis Morlan, at which point, the name changed to Ruby's Dagwood Café.[329] For all its life, the restaurant served up breakfast, blue-plate specials, Italian steak sandwiches, fried tenderloins and hamburgers.

Given that 1117 Southwest Boulevard sits parallel to Turkey Creek and is close to the Kansas River, Dagwood's Café received most of its press coverage during times of flooding, which were frequent and sometimes devastating. Nonetheless, hardship creates iron bonds in a community, and each time flooding happens, the Rosedale neighbors are there to donate, pitch in and bring the restaurant back to life. After the October 1998 flood, the neighbors helped Ruby carry through with her intention to open the café to the homeless

Dagwood's as it appeared in 2021. *Author's photograph.*

for a Thanksgiving dinner. Volunteers sliced onions, peeled potatoes, prepared cranberry relish, baked pumpkin pies and roasted turkeys.

Dennis Morlan passed in 2005, and Ruby sold the café to Greg Hubler in 2010. Hubler does not tamper with tradition. Highly regarded menu items include the beloved Dagwood, created by Ruby's son who requested hash browns on his egg sandwich, along with bacon, sausage (or both) and cheese.[330] Grilled Texas toast encases the fillings. Dagwood's remains one of the few places where diners can also enjoy hot roast beef sandwiches. Those, along with malted waffles, biscuits and gravy, corned beef hash and tenderloin sandwiches consistently make customers forget that it is 2022.

Jess and Jim's Steak House, 1938

517 EAST 135TH STREET
MARTIN CITY (KANSAS CITY), MO

Jess & Jim's Steakhouse continues to reign supreme among carnivores. Calvin Trillin praised this restaurant in his 1972 *Playboy* magazine article, naming it "the finest steakhouse in the world."[331] It achieved such high regard from Trillin because, like Helen Stroud and the Bryant brothers, the original owners, Jess

Jess and Jim's chopped sirloin with its signature loaded baked potato. *Author's photograph.*

Kincaid and Jim Wright, refused to "dress up" the premises or "fancy up" the food. They simply fabricated and correctly aged their beef and then prepared their steaks with no seasoning so that the beef could speak for itself. Then, and now, the food is served in a friendly dining room free of presumption and distraction. Jess & Jim's, in other words, exemplifies Kansas City's culinary ethos: focus on the food, not the Muzak, not the gimmicks.

Steak was not originally the owners' focus. It began as Jess & Jim's Lunch at 135th and Holmes Streets, where the owners' commitment to good food and fair prices over time turned the restaurant into "Jess & Jim's Steak House."[332] The menu, over the decades, has remained largely unchanged, and unlike most fancy chain steakhouses, Jess & Jim's still offers a massive loaded baked potato, fresh vegetables and bread with all its main courses—rather than run up the cost with an à la carte menu.

Aside from the COVID-19 pandemic, Jess & Jim's has survived extraordinary challenges over its long life, particularly the Ruskin Heights May 1957 tornado, which reduced the original location to rubble. By that point, Kincaid had left the business, and Wright had hired his cousin R.C.

Van Noy. They moved the business to its current location, taking over what had partly been a roller rink built in the early 1900s. When Wright's health failed in the late 1970s, Van Noy took over, and after his death, Van Noy's sons, David and Mike, assumed ownership. Today, Mike and his wife, Debbie Van Noy, and the couple's children operate the restaurant. Their daughter Ashley bakes the favorite desserts, including apple pie and carrot cake. The beef is still largely supplied by Wichita-based Sterling Silver, and the biggest appetites often opt for the "Playboy Strip Steak," named after the Trillin article that made the restaurant famous nationally.

RESTAURANTS THAT OPENED IN THE 1940s

Winstead's, 1940

101 EMANUEL CLEAVER II BOULEVARD
KANSAS CITY, MO

In 1940, Kathryn Winstead, with her sister and brother-in-law, Nelle and Gordon Montgomery, opened Winstead's at 101 Brush Creek Boulevard (now known as Forty-Seventh Street). Winstead's is known for its paper-thin steak burger served in a waxed paper wrapping, and its fountain specials, particularly the Frosty, a chocolate ice cream shake thick enough to eat with a spoon.

Gates Bar-B-Q, 1946

With six locations across the metro area, Gates continues to excel in the traditions established by Arthur Pinkard, Henry Perry's apprentice who "came with the place" when George W. and Arzelia June Smith Gates bought Johnny Thomas's Old Kentuck in 1946 and renamed it Gates Ol' Kentucky. Today, Gates is operated by George and Arzelia's son, Ollie Gates, one of Kansas City's most important philanthropists and successful restaurateurs. The restaurant's signature greeting, "Hi, may I help you?" distinguishes Gates from all other barbecue restaurants in the city (probably the world). While no one meat stands out as being better than the rest (everyone has their favorite) Gates excels with its sauce, routinely voted the city's favorite condiment and one that goes well with all the meats and fries. Thankfully, the sauce is available at area grocery stores and shipped nationwide.

Los Corrals, 1949

409 WEST NINTH STREET
KANSAS CITY, MO

The longest-operating Mexican restaurant in Kansas City was opened at 520 West Fourteenth Street and moved to its current location in 1964. Started by Phillip J. Corral Sr. and his wife, Lola, it was then taken over by the couple's children, James A. Corral and Josephine Corral Cervantes. Currently, it is owned by Stephen Neal, who purchased it in 2012. From the beginning, the restaurant has maintained a reputation for its Kansas City tacos, still sprinkled with Romano cheese, and its egg dishes, particularly the huevos rancheros. The surname of the original owners fits the restaurant's heritage, as it is located roughly a mile from where the stockyards operated.

ICONS OF THE FUTURE: RESTAURANTS THAT OPENED IN THE 1950s

Kitty's Café, 1951

810½ EAST THIRTY-FIRST STREET
KANSAS CITY, MO

Originally started by Paul and Kitty Kawakami and currently owned by Charley Soulivong, Kitty's Café continues to offer its Japanese founders' original take on a pork tenderloin sandwich. Kitty's sandwich is composed of three thin-pounded cutlets, tempura fried and topped with lettuce, tomatoes, pickles and house-made hot sauce.

Mugs Up Root Beer, 1952

700 EAST TWENTY-THIRD STREET SOUTH
INDEPENDENCE, MO

The first Mugs Up Drive-In was opened in Kansas City, Missouri, at 6235 Raytown Road in 1952. Its owner James Heavy quickly franchised his business, and for some decades, Mugs Up Root Beer stands dotted the country. This last

one in the metro area was initially owned by Jon Adlard and was purchased in
1978 by Ann Kendall (now Hinojosa) and Bill Kendall. Ann continues to own
the beloved drive-in, famous for its home-brewed root beer and the loose-meat
Zip Burger, which becomes a Whiz Burger when topped with Cheez Whiz.

Cascone's Italian Restaurant, 1954

3733 NORTH OAK TRAFFICWAY
KANSAS CITY, MO

The Cascone family has long been involved in the restaurant business, dating
back at least to the 1930s, when George, John and Leroy Cascone operated
a café at 548 Gillis Street, and later, in 1949, when Cascone's Stainless
Grill operated at 545 Locust Street. The most famous, long-lived Cascone
Restaurant resides in Kansas City's Northland and continues to create the
same house-made red gravy, ravioli, fettucine, lasagna and cannoli—recipes
and techniques that were handed down from the family matriarch, Jennie
Cascone, whose 2003 obituary praised her as an owner and operator of the
restaurant since its 1954 opening.. For decades, Northlanders have treated
Cascone's as a second home, especially given the hospitality and delicious food
that the Cascone family graciously offers up. Southlanders rely on the newer
Johnny Cascone's in Overland Park, Kansas, for similar food and hospitality.

Jasper's Italian Restaurant, 1954

1201 WEST 103RD STREET
KANSAS CITY, MO

Jasper Mirabile Sr. and his wife, Josephine, opened their restaurant at 405
West Seventy-Fifth Street in the Waldo Neighborhood, taking over the former
Rose's Café. They started modestly with twelve tables but grew to become,
along with the American, a Mobil four-star restaurant. Many Kansas Citians,
including this author, remember Jasper's as having the most elegant of
dining experiences, with its menu selections heavily influenced by northern
Italian and French cuisine. Understanding the shifting cultural norms for
fine dining, however, Jasper Sr. decided to leave Waldo and relocate in 1998

to the restaurant's current address, becoming Jasper's Italian Restaurant & Marco Polo's Italian Market. Although the atmosphere is more casual and the menu is more approachable, Jasper's still reigns supreme as a special-occasion restaurant for many. The oldest, best-selling pasta dish is its lux marinara cream-based Capelli d'Angelo alla Nanni, created by Jasper Sr. over sixty years ago and based on a dish that he and Josephine fell in love with in Italy while doing restaurant research. Today, Jasper Jr. operates the restaurant as its head chef, his brother Leonard manages the restaurant and Jasper Mirabile III and Jordon Mirable also manage the day-to-day operations.

Fritz's Railroad Restaurant, 1954

250 NORTH EIGHTEENTH STREET
KANSAS CITY, KS
AND TWO OTHER LOCATIONS

The Kropf family has been long associated with the restaurant business, starting in the 1920s, when John Kropf opened John's Place in Kansas City, Kansas. After returning from World War II, John's son Fritz and Fritz's wife, Virginia, opened Fritz's Drive-In at Thirty-Second Street and Brown Avenue in Kansas City, Kansas. They then opened a second location, which is still in operation today. Due to a labor shortage, Fritz installed phones at each booth for customers to use to call in their orders. His "skat cat" system—what customers delightedly dubbed a train—delivered food orders. While the original location has closed, Fritz's continues to serve customers at its Kansas City, Kansas, location as well as a location in Shawnee, Kansas, and a third at Crown Center. Its most popular items are its cooked-to-order burgers with grilled onions, crinkle-cut fries and onion rings. Fritz's and Virginia's son, Fred, and his wife, Mary, keep this iconic restaurant going today.

Hayes Hamburger and Chili, 1954

2502 NORTHEAST VIVION ROAD
KANSAS CITY, MO

Twelve stools around the counter, five booths that seat at most two people each, a three-foot-long grill, an under-the-counter dishwasher, a tiny fountain and a closet-sized anteroom make up the establishment that was opened by Louise and Irvin Hayes after they purchased a prefab Valentine Diner and had it constructed at the intersection of Vivion and Antioch Roads. After Irvin passed away, his son and the current owner, Jim, stepped up to carry on the traditions. When Jim retired, longtime employee Aaron Sprink, took over general operations. Hayes's chili recipe dates to 1905–6 and comes from Irvin's father, Marvin. That chili and the irresistible one-eighth-of-a-pound burgers, smashed on the griddle with thinly sliced onions, are top sellers, as is the chili cheeseburger.

André's Confiserie Suisse, 1955

5018 Main Street
Kansas City, MO
And One Other Location

Master Konditor-Confiseur André Bollier, his wife, Elsbeth, and their children immigrated to Kansas City in June 1955 and started their Confiserie in October that same year. André's and Elsbeth's children and grandchildren apprenticed and worked in the business. Their daughter Brigitte and son Marcel, with his wife, Connie, as well as their grandson René Bollier trained in Switzerland, and they remain leaders in the business today. Currently, André's daughter Brigitte and her husband, Kevin, operate the store in Overland Park, and their grandson René Bollier and his wife, Nancy, operate the flagship store, now in its third generation. While the hand-made chocolate creations and pastries are exquisite, Andre's is just as famous for its distinctive Swiss chalet–style dining. Each day features a special, ranging from szegediner goulash to croute appenzell, served with Swiss-German salads and a petite pastry.

In-A-Tub, 1955

4000 North Oak Trafficway
Kansas City, MO

In-A-Tub began when Marion and Walt Carpenter opened an ice cream kiosk at 4159 North Oak Trafficway. By 1957, the Carpenters began adding the savory treats that the restaurant is known for, and they settled on the name In-A-Tub. The Carpenters moved their drive-in to a nearby location at 3721 North Oak Trafficway, and then in 1986, Joe Scruby, the second owner, built its third incarnation, where it resides today. When Joe retired, his son, Mike, took over, and when Mike retired in 2001, he sold it to Aaron Beeman, who carries on the tradition today. This unassuming restaurant specializes in the Kansas City taco discussed at length in chapter 7. Also loved are its loose meat "pocket burgers," topped with melty American cheese. Most of the supplies are locally sourced. A second, newer In-A-Tub resides at 8174 Northwest Prairie View Road.

Honorable Mentions (Opened Between 1956–1963)

Snead's Bar-B-Q, Opened Since 1956

1001 East 171st Street
Belton, MO

HiBoy Drive-In, Opened Since 1957

3424 South Blue Ridge Cut Off
Independence, MO

Humdinger Drive-In, Opened Since 1962

2504 East Ninth Street
Kansas City, MO

El Sombrero Mexican Restaurant, Opened Since 1963

79 East 69 Highway
Kansas City, MO

V's Italiano Ristorante, Opened Since 1963

10819 East U.S. Highway 40
Independence, MO.

Notes

Chapter 1

1. Many sources give this history in detail, including Andrea Broomfield, *Kansas City: A Food Biography* (Lanham, MD: Rowman & Littlefield, 2016) and James Shortridge, *Kansas City and How It Grew, 1822–2011* (Lawrence: University of Kansas Press, 2012).
2. Broomfield, *Food Biography*, 7–8.
3. Nellie McCoy Harris, "Memories of Old Westport," *Annals of Kansas City* 1, no. 4 (1924): 471–72, 474; see also William Barnard, "Westport and the Santa Fe Trade," in *Transactions of the Kansas State Historical Society*, vol. 9 (Topeka, KS: State Printing Office, 1906), 553–65, www.archive.org.
4. Edward R. Schauffler, "Westport's No. 1 Romance," *Swing*, November 1945, 37–40.
5. Barnard, "Westport," 9.
6. Information on the history of the plot pre–Harris House can be contradictory. The best source is: Vertical file, Hotels, "Gillis House," Kansas City Public Library, Missouri Valley Special Collections.
7. Carrie Westlake Whitney, *Kansas City, Missouri: Its History and Its People, 1808–1903*, vol. 1 (Chicago: S.J. Clarke Publishing, 1908), 651; Harris, "Memories," 471–72, 474; "Mark Harris House Site," *Kansas City Star*, June 13, 1926, 12.
8. "Harris House Site," *Kansas City Star*, 12.
9. Whitney, *Kansas City, Missouri*, 1:651.

10. "Harris House and Its Cookery to Be Preserved," *Kansas City Star*, June 25, 1912, 4.

11. "Old Harris House Is Sold," *Kansas City Star*, July 23, 1822, D:9; David R. Baumgartner, "Hey Ma, What's for Dinner?" *Kansas City Magazine*, February 2001, 31–34.

12. Broomfield, *Food Biography*, 54.

13. Quoted in A. Theodore Brown, *Frontier Community: Kansas City to 1870* (Columbia: University of Missouri Press, 1863), 101; see also, Theodore S. Case, *History of Kanas City, Missouri* (Syracuse, NY: D. Mason & Co., 1888), 55.

14. "We Found Out," *Kansas City Star*, June 25, 1950, D:6.

15. Henry Van Brunt, "Hotels Had a Shining Era Here During Push West," *Kansas City Star*, June 25, 1950, C:1.

16. "Gillis House Hotel was a Prison in 1864," *Kansas City Genealogist* 40, no. 3 (2000): 104; Brown, *Frontier Community*, 54.

17. Alan W. Farley, "Annals of Quindaro: A Kansas Ghost Town," *Kansas Historical Quarterly* 22, no. 4 (1956): 305–20, www.kancoll.org.

18. Rick Montgomery and Shirl Kasper, *Kansas City: An American Story* (Kansas City, MO: Kansas City Star Books, 1999), 46; "Local Matters," *Quindaro Chindowan*, January 23, 1858.

19. Farley, "Annals of Quindaro," 305–20.

20. "On Board the Cataract, Missouri River, Wednesday, Aug. 19, 1857," *Western Home Journal* (Lawrence, KS), August 27, 1875; "On the Wing," *Kanzas News* (Emporia, KS), December 12, 1857.

21. "Thanksgiving," *Quindaro Chindowan*, November 28, 1857.

Chapter 2

22. Stephen Fried, *Appetite for America: How Visionary Businessman Fred Harvey Built a Railroad Hospitality Empire That Civilized the Wild West* (New York: Random House, 2011), 231, 296.

23. Shortridge, *Kansas City*, 25.

24. "Broadway Hotel," *Kansas City Times*, April 23, 1873, 4; "Coates House," *Kansas City Times*, May 18, 1873, 4.

25. Vertical file, "Coates House Hotel," Missouri Valley Special Collections, Kansas City Public Library; Shortridge, *Kansas City*, 50.

26. David S. Shields, *The Culinarians: Lives and Careers from the First Age of American Fine Dining* (Chicago: Chicago University Press, 2017), 478–80.

27. Advertisement, *Independent*, February 27, 1915; Broomfield, *Food Biography*, 125.

28. "Santa Fe Trail Frieze," *Kansas City Star*, December 17, 1905, 1.

29. Broomfield, *Food Biography*, 126–27.

30. Charles Ferruzza, "A Savvy Savoy," *Pitch*, September 12, 2002, www. thepitchkc.com.

31. Author's interview with Jack Holland, August 28, 2019.

32. Fred Harvey breakfast menu, Joe Maciel Menu Collection; Vertical file, Edna Binkley Collection, Kansas City Museum and Union Station; "Restaurants-Harvey House," Missouri Valley Special Collections, Kansas City Public Library.

33. "Success Is More Than a Belt Size," *Kansas City Times*, April 17, 1982, B:1; "Fred Harvey Closing Marks End of Era," *Kansas City Times*, December 28, 1968, C:12.

34. "Westport Room," *Kansas Citian*, November 4, 1958, 21.

35. "Fred Harvey Closing," *Kansas City Times*, December 28, 1968, C:12.

36. Author's interview with Joseph William "Bill" Gilbert, April 25, 2015.

37. "Joe Gilbert Would Get Airport Concession," *Kansas City Times*, December 19, 1958, A:4.

38. "Dining, Drinking, and All That Jazz," *Kansas City Star*, June 14, 1964, F:7.

39. Author's interview with Jay Huey, December 16, 2019.

40. Frank Driggs and Chuck Haddix, *Kansas City Jazz: From Ragtime to Bebop* (Oxford: Oxford University Press, 2005), 245; Broomfield, *Food Biography*, 128.

41. National Register of Historic Places, U.S. Department of the Interior, "Downtown Hotels in Kansas City, Missouri," Inventory Nomination Form, July 1982, www.dnr.mo.gov.

42. "Work on Hotel Grill," *Kansas City Star*, November 6, 1938, D:3.

43. Author's interview with Jess Barbosa, March 27, 2015; Author's interview with Jesse John Vega Sr., July 20, 2020.

44. Buck O'Neil, with Steve Wulf and David Conrads, *I Was Right on Time: My Journey from the Negro Leagues to the Majors* (New York: Simon & Schuster, 1996), 75.

45. Tina Cahalan Jones, "Reuben and Ella Davison Street and Their Kansas City Blue Room," *From Slaves to Soldiers and Beyond—Williamson County Tennessee's African American History*, March 8, 2019, www.usctwillcotn. blogspot.com.

46. Broomfield, *Food Biography*, 97.

47. "New Streets Hotel Attracts Keen Interest," *Kansas City Call*, December 9, 1949, 24.

48. Ibid.

49. Jones, "Reuben and Ella Davison Street."

50. Chuck Haddix, email to the author, November 7, 2019.

51. "Hopes, Dreams, History and Music Haunt 18th and Vine," *Kansas City Star*, February 8, 1992, E:1.

52. "New Streets Hotel," *Kansas City Call*, n.p.

53. O'Neil, *I Was Right on Time*, 75.

54. Boots Mathews and James Rieger, *Dining In: Kansas City* (Mercer Island, Washington: Peanut Butter Publishing, 1983), 2; *Clarendon Guide to Kansas City Restaurants* (Memphis, TN: C&S Enterprises, 1982), 42.

55. Debora Bowman, "Alameda Rooftop, Kansas City Memories," Facebook, June 10, 2015, www.facebook.com.

56. Kurt Grunwald, "Pam Pam West, Kansas City Memories," Facebook, November 19, 2020, www.facebook.com; Shifra Stein, *Edible City: Restaurants & Their Recipes* (Kansas City, MO: Flying Owl, 1978), 23.

57. "Nichols Trades Independence for More Cash, Less Risk," *Kansas City Business Journal*, March 19, 1990, 10; Kurt Fahey, "Alameda Hotel, Kansas City Memories," Facebook, June 10, 2015, www.facebook.com.

58. "For Ducks or Desserts, Try the Peppercorn," *Kansas City Times*, October 9, 1985, D:3.

59. "At the Club," *Pitch*, February 14, 2008, www.thepitchkc.com.

60. Author's interview with Charles Broomfield, February 10, 2020.

61. "Grim Days Kept in Background at Subdued, Optimistic Opening," *Kansas City Star*, October 2, 1891, A:9.

62. "At the Club," *Pitch*.

Chapter 3

63. "Kansas City Ports of Call," *Swing*, January 1945, 5.

64. Matt Gilligan, "Home Cookin' at the Green Parrot Inn," *Johnson County Museum*, November 12, 2014, www.jocohistory.wordpress.com; Mrs. Sam Ray Postcard Collection (SC58), Kansas City Public Library, Missouri Valley Special Collections.

65. Mathews and Rieger, *Dining In*, 164.

66. "End of Green Rice, Fritters," *Kansas City Star*, February 16, 2007, B:1.

67. Mathews and Rieger, *Dining In*, 64.

68. Jasper Mirable, "Remembering Stephenson's Apple Farm," *Kansas City Star*, April 20, 2016, *www.newsbank.com*.

69. "Why All the Fanfare?" *Kansas City Star*, July 4, 2006, D:1; "Born on a Wing and a Wishbone," *Kansas City Star*, August 7, 1996, E:1; James Dornbrook, "Wish-Bone History Tied to Kansas City, "*Kansas City Business Journal*, August 14, 2013.

70. Quoted in Jacquie Lehatto, "Resolve, Refinement Central to Her," *Kansas City Star*, November 27, 2007.

71. "True American Dining at the Wishbone," *This Month in Kansas City* (March 1972), 25; Mary Accurso Dodd, "Wishbone, Kansas City Memories," Facebook, January 20, 2019, www.facebook.com.

72. "Historic House of Kansas Restored as Tea Room," *Kansas City Star*, January 25, 1953, C:2.

73. "Grinter Place," transcript of an unpublished manual created by Rodney Staab, curator of the Grinter Place Historic Site, 1986–97, transcribed by Swiftwater Thomas F. Hahn, editor, Lenape-Delaware History, November 20, 2006, www.lenapedelawarehistory.net.

74. "Historic House of Kansas Restored as Tea Room," *Kansas City Star*, January 25, 1953, C:2.

75. Eleanor Richey Johnston and Bernice Hanson, *Old Grinter House Cook Book* (Lawrence, KS: Allen Press, 1953), iii.

76. Broomfield, *Food Biography*, 142.

77. National Register of Historic Places, U.S. Department of the Interior, "Oak Ridge Tea House Manor," Inventory Nomination Form, July 1982, www.dnr.mo.gov.

78. Ibid.

79. "John E. Peter," *Kansas City Times*, July 7, 1970, 15; Zesto Franchising, "History," www.zestofranchising.com; "Peter's Drive-In Retains a Taste of the Flavorful 50s," *Kansas City Times*, October 16, 1976, A:19.

80. Cait McKnelly, "Peter's Drive-In, Things and Places in Greater Kansas City," Facebook, March 10, 2020, www.facebook.com.

81. "Bernadine C. Peter," *Kansas City Star*, July 26, 1994, B:3.

82. Find a Grave, "Alice 'Nadine' Baker, Obituary, 1926–2013," www.findagrave.com.

83. Author's interview with Wesley T. and Susan Fielder, May 3, 2020.

84. Patricia Jones, "Allen's Drive-In, Kansas City Memories," Facebook, April 13, 2020.

85. Fielder interview, May 3, 2020.

86. Author's interview with Julie Haas, May 11, 2020; "Kansas City Ports of Call," *Swing*, January 1948, 67.

87. Fielder interview, May 3, 2020.

88. The first job advertisement for Smaks that the author discovered is dated September 7, 1954, in the *Kansas City Times*. See also "Rugel Drive-In Units Are Sold," *Kansas City Star*, May 25, 1958, D:6.

89. Jonathan Bender, "Whatever Happened to Smaks?" *Flatland*, October 9, 2017, www.flatlandkc.org.

90. Aaron Baar, "Bernstein-Rein, Big Mac United," *Adweek*, August 10, 1998, www.adweek.com; "KC Marketer Behind Happy Meals' Success," *Lawrence Journal-World*, August 14, 2004, www2.ljworld.com.

91. "Bank to Replace Allen's," *Kansas City Star*, February 12, 1978.

92. "Sidney's On the Block Today," *Kansas City Times*, September 24, 1974, 3.

93. "Drinking, Dining, and All That Jazz," *Kansas City Star*, June 13, 1965, E:6.

94. "Sidney's Restaurant Tie in 320-Acre Farm Deal," *Kansas City Star*, June 6, 1965, D:6.

95. Alexis Harmon, "Sydney's Drive-In, Kansas City: Lost Drive-Ins and Cafes," Facebook, November 24, 2017, www.facebook.com.

96. "Sidney's On the Block Today," *Kansas City Times*, 3.

Chapter 4

97. Daniel Coleman, "Biography of Henry Perry," Kansas City History, 2005, www.kchistory.org.

98. My thanks to Missouri Valley Special Collections archive librarian Michael Wells for drawing this article to my attention. See "How 'Henery' Perry Got the Title and Keeps It," *Kansas City Star*, January 17, 1911, 14.

99. "How 'Henery' Perry Got the Title," *Kansas City Star*, 14.

100. Michael Wells, email to the author, July 15, 2021; "Birthday Dinner," *Kansas City Sun*, December 9, 1916, 1.

101. Author's interview with Sonny Gibson, February 15, 2020.

102. "Henry Perry Has Cooked Good Barbecue for 50 Years," *Kansas City Call*, February 26, 1932.

103. Catherine Neville, "The Kings of Kansas City Barbecue," *Feast*, August 25, 2017, www.feastmagazine.com.

104. Stanley Crouch, *Kansas City Lightning: The Rise and Times of Charlie Parker* (New York: HarperCollins, 2013), 188.

105. Ross Russell, *Jazz Style in Kansas City and the Southwest* (Berkeley: University of California Press, 1971) 21.

106. Eric Elie Lolis and Frank Stewart, *Smokestack Lightning: Adventures in the Heart of Barbecue Country* (Berkeley, CA: Ten Speed Press, 1996), 145.

107. Connie McCabe, "KC BBQ," *Saveur*, May 21, 2007, www.saveur.com.

108. "Otis P. Boyd," *Kansas City Star*, January 31, 1999, B:4.

109. Lolis and Stewart, *Smokestack Lightning*, 146.

110. Doug Worgul, *Grand Barbecue: A Celebration of the History, Places, Personalities and Techniques of Kansas City Barbecue* (Kansas City, MO: Kansas City Star Books, 2002), 47; Terri Baumgartner, "Cookin' with the Blues," *Kansas City Star*, May 3, 1998, 19.

111. "Down to the Bar BQ," audio CD, track 3, on *Original Blues*, Shakehouse Records, 2010.

112. Doug Worgul, "Saving the Soul of a City," *Kansas City Star*, January 2, 2000, 11.

113. Author's interview with Glenn Patrik, February 16, 2020.

114. Ibid.

115. Baumgartner, "Cookin' with the Blues," 19.

116. Author's interview with Ron Quick, February 20, 2020.

117. Ibid.

118. "Barbecue 'Oklahoma Tenderloin' Hard to Find in KC—That's No Baloney," *Kansas City Star*, January 23, 2014.

119. "Quick's Bar-B-Q Closes Today after 50 Years in Kansas City," *Pitch*, November 7, 2014, www.thepitchkc.com.

120. Betty Fussell, *Raising Steaks: The Life and Times of American Beef* (Boston: Harcourt, 2008), 297.

121. "Sizzle Is Gone for Landmark Steak House," *Kansas City Business Journal*, October 28, 1994, 1.

122. Ibid.

123. Ibid.

124. "About Town," *Kansas City Times*, April 18, 1961, 25.

125. "Tudie Lusco Fondly Recalls '30s," *Kansas City Times*, June 30, 1973, A:16.

126. Emma Lee Holley had planned to reopen the restaurant with the same name and décor, but in July 1981, the building caught fire. The structure was razed.

127. KCUR, "Golden Ox, A Piece of Kansas City's Cowtown Past, Set to Close," Kansas City Public Radio, December 19, 2014, www.kcur.org.

128. J'Nell L. Pate, *America's Historic Stockyards: Livestock Hotels* (Fort Worth: Texas Christian University Press, 2005), 91.

129. Jane Stern and Michael Stern, *Roadfood* (New York: Broadway Books, 2005), 367; "Golden Ox: Still No Bull," *Pitch*, May 7, 2009, www.thepitchkc.com.

130. Victor L. Anfuso, "Main Splendor at the Golden Ox," *Congressional Record: Proceedings and Debates of the 87ᵗʰ Congress, Second Session* 108, no. 17 (October 5, 1962–October 13, 1962): 23,268; Robert Shoffner, "Washington Dining: JFK Knew Good Food," *Washington Post*, October 1, 2005, www.washingtonian.com.

131. "Golden Ox Co-Owner Steve Greer Is Ready to Un-Retire," *Pitch*, December 2, 2014, www.thepitchkc.com.

132. KCUR, "Kansas City Masterpieces," Kansas City Public Radio, January 5, 2016, www.kcur.org.

133. The original Golden Ox restaurant space is shared with the Stockyards Brewing Co. as of 2021.

134. Author's interview with Karen Gaines, January 20, 2019.

135. "Lost Colony," *Pitch*, December 7, 2000, www.thepitchkc.com.

136. Gaines interview, January 20, 2019.

137. Greg Borzo, *Lost Restaurants of Chicago* (Charleston: The History Press, 2018), 7.

138. Author's interview with Ted B. Meadows, July 21, 2021.

139. Quoted in "60-Year Run Comes to Close at Frontier Steakhouse," *Wyandotte Daily*, December 11, 2020, www.wyandottedaily.com.

Chapter 5

140. "Going Out," *Kansas City Times*, February 20, 1976, A:14.

141. "Best of the Century are Chosen," *Squire*, August 2005, 1–3.

142. Quoted in Jane P. Fowler, "New Bretton's Helmsman, but Max Is Still On Board," *Kansas City Star*, September 17, 1972, C:2.

143. "Kansas City's Ports of Call," *Swing*, May 1947, 66; "Soup Days," *Pitch*, April 19, 2001, www.thepitchkc.com; Author's interview with Deborah Bretton Granoff, June 26, 2021.

144. Quoted in Fowler, "New Bretton's Helmsman," C:2.

145. Author's interview with Charles Broomfield, September 28, 2021.

146. *City Divided: The Racial Landscape of Kansas City, 1900–1960* (Columbia: University of Missouri Press, 2002), 200.

147. "The Gift to See," *Kansas City Star*, March 27, 1979, G:3.

148. "It Happened in Kansas City," *Kansas City Star*, March 23, 1947, A:2.

149. Author's interview with Mary Sanchez, July 17, 2020.

150. "Remembering Putsch's 210," *Pitch*, June 21, 2010, www.thepitchkc.com.

151. "Restaurant's End Evokes Family History," *Kansas City Star*, September 23, 2003, B:5.

152. "About Town," *Kansas City Times*, April 16, 1965, 35.

153. Ibid.

154. Author's interview with Jim Eddy, July 15, 2020.

155. Rob Roberts, "13th and Baltimore—An Intersection in Time," *Kansas City Business Journal*, September 5, 2014, www.bizjournals.com.

156. "New Downtown Restaurant Copies Car Seat for Booths," *Kansas City Star*, February 6, 1949, D:8.

157. "A Feast for You, a Break for Your Wallet," *Kansas City Star*, July 17, 1992, H:26; "Dining Out," *Town Squire*, December 1981, 82–84.

158. "French Couple's Cuisine Secret to Instant Success," *Kansas City Star*, February 20, 1972, C:7.

159. Ibid.

160. *Clarendon Guide*, 112–15.

161. Quoted in John Martellaro, "Romance à la Carte," *Kansas City Star*, February 13, 1991, E:7.

162. "Plaza Restaurants on Move: La Mediterranee and House of Toy Not Pleased by Changes," *Kansas City Star*, March 5, 1993, B:3.

163. "Restaurants See Suburban Boon," *Kansas City Star*, November 30, 1994, B:3.

164. "The Med Is Back—and the Food Is Still Inspired," *Kansas City Star*, May 11, 1994, G:29.

165. "American Wins 2018 Design Icon James Beard Award," *Feast*, March 13, 2018, www.feastmagazine.com.

166. "Nothing 'Pseudo' to Be Served," *Kansas City Star*, January 20, 1974, F:10.

167. "American Hero," *Ingram's*, March 1992, 38.

168. Ibid.

169. "Under New Chefs, the Grand American Is Even Grander," *Kansas City Star*, August 19, 1994, G:29.

170. Author's interview with Michael Smith, October 19, 2020.

171. "It's a Real Compliment to the Chefs," *Kansas City Star*, April 2, 1997, F:1; "Under New Chefs," *Kansas City Star*, G:29.

172. "A Star Is Reborn," *Kansas City Star*, February 10, 2019, 53.

173. Smith interview, October 19, 2020.

174. "French Dis," *Pitch*, July 19, 2001, www.thepitchkc.com.

175. Ken Frydman, "Gilbert/Robinson Positioning Fedora as New Growth Vehicle," *Nation's Restaurant News*, March 24, 1986, 1.

176. Jesse John Vega Sr., email to the author, November 12, 2020.

177. Frydman, "Gilbert/Robinson Positioning Fedora," 1.

178. David Davis, email to the author, July 28, 2021.

179. "French Dis," *Pitch.*

180. Steve Cole, email to the author, November 4, 2020.

181. "KC Restaurants Pop Corks on Wine-Preserving Systems," *Kansas City Times*, February 11, 1987, C:11.

182. "Café Allegro Upholds Its New American Reputation," *Kansas City Star*, October 2, 1998, 39.

183. "Master in the Art of Fine Food," *Kansas City Star*, August 20, 1992, C:1.

184. "Part-Time Caterer Whips Up Meals for KC Rescue Mission," *Kansas City Star*, December 23, 1990, E:4.

Chapter 6

185. "Myron Green Turned from Dentistry to Restaurants," *Kansas City Star*, July 6, 1930, C:6; David Conrads, "Biography of Myron Green (1876–1953), Restaurateur," Missouri Valley Special Collections: Biography, Kansas City Public Library, 1999, www.kchistory.org.

186. Samantha Barbas, "Just Like Home: 'Home Cooking' and the Domestication of the American Restaurant," *Gastronomica* 2, no. 4 (2002): 43–52.

187. Dick Fowler, *Leaders in Our Town* (Kansas City, MO: Burd & Fletcher, n.d.), 187.

188. Ibid.

189. "Clem T. Templin," *Kansas City Times*, June 15, 1966, 23.

190. Fowler, *Leaders*, 188.

191. "Fifty Years Ago: July 10 through 16th," *Examiner* (Kansas City, MO), July 17, 2010, www.examiner.net; "Restaurants End K.C. Bias," *Pittsburgh Courier*, July 30, 1960, 29.

192. Schirmer, *City Divided*, 200.

193. "Buy Martin's On the Plaza: Mr. and Mrs. J.W. Putsch, New Owners of Cafeteria," *Kansas City Star*, March 17, 1946, D:8; "Mrs. Putsch Dies," *Kansas City Star*, March 31, 1972, 22.

194. David Conrads, "Justus W. Putsch: Restaurateur," Missouri Valley Special Collections, Kansas City Public Library, 1999, www.kchistory.org.

195. "From Days Gone By, a Tradition Worth Keeping," *Kansas City Star*, December 25, 2007, B:7, www.newsbank.com.

196. Driggs and Haddix, *Kansas City Jazz*, 137.

197. Dan Margolies, "Sanderson's Owner to Take His Tenderloins to South KC," *Kansas City Business Journal*, June 27, 1999, www.bizjournals.com.

198. Author's interview with Charles Broomfield, July 12, 2020.

199. Quoted in Art Lamb, *Sanderson's Lunch* (Leawood, KS: Leather's Publishing, 1998), 4. Subsequent information on Art Lamb's ownership of Sanderson's comes from *Sanderson's Lunch*.

200. "William B. Sanderson," *Kansas City Times*, April 26, 1974, 29.

201. "Famous Eatery Closes Its Doors," *Kansas City Star*, May 26, 2000, sec. C, 2.

202. "Here Come the Regulars," *Kansas City Star*, September 19, 1996, 12.

203. John Mariani, *America Eats Out* (New York: William Morrow, 1991), 70.

204. "Here Come the Regulars," *Kansas City Star*, 12.

205. Ibid.

206. "Capote Over Easy," *Pitch*, February 9, 2006, www.thepitchkc.com.

207. "Historical Perspective: Jacob Bauer Still Recognized as 'Father of the Soda Fountain,'" *Tribune-Star* (Terre Haute, IN), July 3, 2010, www.tribstar.com.

208. Jason Roe, "Katz in the Cradle," *This Week in Kansas City History*, Kansas City Public Library, www.kchistory.org.

209. Jan Dumay, "Enduring Legacy of Katz Drug Stores," *Kansas City Magazine*, August 11, 2014, www.kansascitymag.com.

210. Dan Anderson, "A Lunch Counter?" *Food Tells a Story*, February 10, 2016, www.foodtellsastory.wordpress.com.

211. Mary Kimbrough and Margaret W. Dagen, *Victory Without Violence: The First Ten Years of the St. Louis Committee of Racial Equality (CORE)* (Columbia: University of Missouri Press, 2000), 61–62; Jean Van Delinder, *Struggles Before Brown: Early Civil Rights Protests and Their Significance Today* (New York: Routledge, 2015), 125.

212. "Ruby McIntyre, Remembered for Soul Food Café, Dies at 95," *Kansas City Star*, May 14, 2015, A:4.

213. Sally Barth and John Kiely, "Student Pictures of Ruby," *Hatebusters*, May 19, 2015, www.hatebusters.wordpress.com; Ed Chasteen, "Ruby's Soul Food Café," *Hatebusters*, May 19, 2015, www.hatebusters.wordpress.com; Jan Smith, "Ruby's: No Brass or Plants, Just Good Ol' Soul Food," *Kansas City Magazine*, February 1985, 18; "Favorite Friends Feast at Ruby's Reopening," *Kansas City Star*, November 13, 1977, A:48.

214. "After 40 Years, Ruby Still Rules and the Food Is Still Fabulous," *Kansas City Star*, December 16, 1994, B:3.

215. "Ruby Will Serve No Tears When Restaurant Closes," *Kansas City Star*, May 24, 2001, E:4.

216. Ed Chasteen, "1987," *Hatebusters*, May 19, 2015, www.hatebusters.wordpress.com.

217. Facebook, "Tribute to Ruby McIntyre, Joe's Kansas City," May 12, 2015, www.facebook.com.

218. The Royals played at Municipal Stadium from 1969 to 1972, and the Chiefs played there from 1963 to 1971.

219. Carla Labat, *Satisfy Your Soul: A Guide to African American, African & Caribbean Restaurants* (McClean, VA: Impressions Books, 1997), 84.

220. Melissa Bedford, "These Good Soul Cooks Know Food," *Kansas City Star*, November 19, 1995, 9.

221. Ibid.

222. "Ruby and Maxine Keep Spirit of Soul Alive," *Kansas City Star*, February 22, 2002, 26.

223. Michael MacCambridge, *'69 Chiefs: A Team, A Season, and the Birth of Modern Kansas City* (Kansas City, MO: Andrews McMeel, 2019), 89.

224. "Trying to Move On, Trying to Remember," *Seattle Times*, October 2, 2000, www.archive.seattletimes.com.

225. "A Song for Fallen Friends," *Kansas City Star*, January 26, 2002, E:1.

Chapter 7

226. "Mex to the Max," *Ingram's*, March 1997, 46.

227. Author's interview with Suzanne Lozano, December 10, 2021.

228. "Ports of Call: KC," *Swing*, October 1945, 57.

229. Suzanne Infante Lozano, email to the author, August 9, 2021; Jose R. Ralat, "The Demand for 'Authenticity' Is Threatening Kansas City's Homegrown Tacos," *Eater*, April 23, 2019, www.eater.com.

230. Suzanne Infante Lozano, email to author, August 9, 2021.

231. Author's interview with Jeanie Barrera, December 16, 2020.

232. "Enchiladas Suizas," *Saveur*, July 17, 2012, www.saveur.com.

233. "Dining In—and Out," *Kansas City Star*, May 7, 1967, D:2.

234. Ibid., D:2; "Augustin 'Gus' Ibarra," *Kansas City Star*, July 8, 2015, A:14.

235. "Dining In—and Out," *Kansas City Star*, D-7.

236. Walt Bodine, *What Do You Say to That?* (Kansas City, MO: Westport Publishers, 1988), 71–72.

237. "By Hard Work They Made Good," *Kansas City Times*, February 20, 1978, B:6.

238. Ibid.

239. "Jessie C. Rodriguez," *Kansas City Times*, October 10, 1988, B:7.

240. Jesse John Vega Sr., email to the author, February 8, 2021; Ted Palmer, "Famous Mexican Restaurant in City Market," *Dos Mundos*, July 9, 1998.

241. Dennis Shmania, "Molina's, Things and Places We Loved in Greater KC," Facebook, October 27, 2020, www.facebook.com.

242. Vega email, February 8, 2021.

243. "Mrs. Guadalupe Garcia," *Kansas City Times*, June 10, 1977, 11.

244. Author's interview with Donald Quinn II, January 8, 2021.

245. "Christmas Flavored Mexican Style," *Kansas City Star*, December 20, 1970, C:20.

246. Quinn interview, January 8, 2021.

247. Author's interview with Kathy Quinn, January 4, 2021.

Chapter 8

248. Shortridge, *Kansas City*, 91; Hasia R. Diner, *Hungering for America: Italian, Irish, and Jewish Foodways in the Age of Migration* (Cambridge, MA: Harvard University Press, 2001), 34, 43.

249. See "Talkfest with Spaghetti," *Kansas City Times*, February 13, 1908, 12.

250. Matt Sterns, "An Evolving Menu," *Kansas City Star*, May 23, 2001, 8

251. KCUR, "Finding a Great Sandwich," Kansas City Public Radio, April 5, 2012, www.kcur.org.

252. Carl J. DiCapo, John David DiCapo and Frank R. Hyde, *Italian Gardens: A History of Kansas City through Its Favorite Restaurant* (place of publication: Carl DiCapo, 2010), xi, 4. The quotations and historical details that follow in this section come from this particular book.

253. "Restaurants Aplenty," *Kansas City Star*, June 17, 1990, 70–71.

254. DiCapo, DiCapo and Hyde, *Italian Gardens*, 28.

255. Ibid., 175.

256. Ibid., 159–60.

257. "3-Generation Baptismal Gown," *Kansas City Times*, February 1, 1961, 17.

258. "Ports of Call, KC," *Swing*, February 1947, 65.

259. "Food Was a Love Affair," *Kansas City Times*, August 3, 1972, A:12.

260. "Dining, Drinking, and All That Jazz," *Kansas City Star*, July 26, 1964, D:3; Danny Costello, "Il Pagliaccio, Lost Drive-Ins and Cafés," Facebook, March 1, 2021, www.facebook.com.

261. "Cronies Salute Old M.U. No. 32," *Kansas City Times*, November 25, 1976, D:21.

262. Author's interview with Santamary Lozano, July 19, 2020; Author's interview with Vincent Miller, October 23, 2021.

263. "Dining, Drinking, and All That Jazz," *Kansas City Star*, September 5, 1965, E:4.

264. Lozano interview, July 19, 2020.

265. *Clarendon Guide*, 84.

266. "Restaurant into New Apartment Building," *Kansas City Star*, July 20, 1969, E:6.

267. "Menus for All Tastes," *Kansas City Star*, December 1, 1974, E:10.

268. *Clarendon Guide*, 84.

269. "Sporting Comment," *Kansas City Star*, July 27, 1971, 11.

270. Quoted in "Pizza Wars," *Kansas City Star*, November 17, 1986, C:1.

271. "Saucy Meatball Secret to Delicatessen's Success," *Kansas City Star*, January 17, 1971, C:7.

272. Edward DeBlasio, "The Big Bite," *Hartford Courant Magazine*, July 30, 1950, 6.

273. "Sandwiches: Making the Most of a Good Thing," *New York Times*, August 11, 1982, www.nytimes.com.

274. "Plaza Restaurants Recover from the Flood," *Kansas City Star*, December 22, 1977, 7; "Plaza Suffers Flood and Fire Havoc," *Kansas City Star*, September 13, 1977, 11.

275. Author's interview with Allison Smith, August 18, 2021; *Clarendon Guide*, 126–27.

276. "A (Mostly) Successful Update of Italian Cuisine," *Kansas City Star*, November 22, 1991, G:25.

277. "Discotheque Adds Dimension to Restaurant," *Kansas City Star*, June 23, 1976, B:5.

278. Ibid.

279. "Victor Victorious," *Pitch*, June 26, 2003, www.thepitchkc.com.

280. "Discotheque Adds Dimension," *Kansas City Star*, B:5.

281. "Fanny's Restaurant...Chic and Low-Key," *Kansas City Times*, August 26, 1977, B:5.

282. Author's interview with Lazer Avery, May 10, 2021.

283. Ibid.

284. Ibid.; Natalie Torres Gallagher, "Chicken Spiedini Is a KC Icon," *Kansas City Magazine*, April 27, 2021, www.kansascitymag.com.

285. Both Fanny's menu and the American's are included in Robert C. Mortimer and Charles C. Mortimer's *Menu Guide of Kansas City* (Pacific Palisades, CA: Corm Enterprises, 1976), 6, 35.

Chapter 9

286. Broomfield, *Food Biography*, 65.

287. "Frank X. Wachter Dies," *Kansas City Times*, May 4, 1940, 8.

288. "About Town," *Kansas City Times*, August 25, 1964, 25.

289. "It Happened in Kansas City," *Kansas City Star*, May 10, 1958, A:10.

290. "Election Strategy for Breakfast," *Kansas City Star*, February 24, 1994, C:1; "Meierhoff's Goes to New Owners," *Kansas City Star*, February 12, 1993, B:3.

291. "Restaurant Damaged in Blaze," *Kansas City Star*, February 23, 1994, C:1.

292. "Escape from Russians Led a Young German to Kansas City," *Kansas City Star*, September 24, 1972, 19.

293. "Dining, Drinking, and All That Jazz," *Kansas City Star*, June 13, 1965, E:6; "Dining, Drinking, and All That Jazz," *Kansas City Star*, June 2, 1976, B:8.

294. "Bye-Bye, Bear," *Pitch*, May 10, 2007, www.thepitchkc.com.

295. Jayne Eggerstedt Johnson, email to the author, June 10, 2021.

296. This biographical information comes from the newspaper obituaries of Esther Lessner Becker, Jacob Lessner and Isadore Becker, as well as early Kansas City Directories made available through www.ancestry.com. See also "A Taste for History," *Kansas City Star*, May 3, 2005, D:1.

297. David Sax, *Save the Deli: In Search of Perfect Pastrami, Crusty Rye, and the Heart of the Jewish Delicatessen* (Toronto: McClell and Stewart, 2009), 112.

298. "What Would Jesus Eat?" *Pitch*, March 26, 2009, www.thepitchkc.com.

299. "Hope You're Hungry," *Kansas City Star*, June 25, 1998, 10.

300. Sax, *Save the Deli*, 111.

301. Find a Grave, "Reltz Lenet," www.findagrave.com; "Izaak Biszkowicz," *Kansas City Times*, May 20, 1964, 20.

302. "New Café to Open Soon," *B'nai B'rith Messenger* (Los Angeles, CA), August 8, 1930, 3, www.nli.org; "Harry Weiss," *Kansas City Times*, November 16, 1965, 24.

303. "Kansas City Ports of Call," *Swing*, February 1946, 63; "Kansas City Ports of Call," *Swing*, November 1946, 60.

304. Phillip Weiss, email to the author, September 4, 2021.

305. "Jennie L. Bukovac," *Kansas City Star*, April 5, 1990, C:4.

306. "Dining at Neighborhood Restaurants," *Kansas City Star*, July 10, 1977, 19; "Jennie's Restaurant on Strawberry Hill Serves Its Last Meal," *Kansas City Star*, November 15, 2000, 7; Mariann Jaksa, email with author, January 16, 2022.

307. "At Jennie's, Food Is Like Grandma Used to Make," *Kansas City Star*, November 12, 1981, B:3.

308. "Restaurants Add Flavor to Kansan Life," *Kansas City Star*, February 21, 1980.

309. Chinese American Museum of Chicago, "Chinese Food and Politics in Chicago, 1905–07," www.ccamuseum.org; "A Rich Chinaman's Bride," *Kansas City Times*, May 31, 1904, 6.

310. "Old Restaurants Never Die," *Kansas City Star*, February 3, 1999.

311. "Grand View of Downtown's Crossroads," *Kansas City Star*, June 8, 2003, 39.

312. House of Toy's history is confusing and, at times, contradictory. The author's information on its ownership comes from the earliest-known article to mention both King Joy Lo and House of Toy, suggesting that House of Toy was initially owned by Don Toy and that his cousin Harry joined him after King Joy Lo closed. See "Chinese New Year Will Arrive with Dignity," *Kansas City Times*, February 15, 1961, 3.

313. *Clarendon Guide*, 99.

314. "Disastrous Flood Couldn't Drown Plaza Restaurants," *Kansas City Times*, August 3, 1979, C:1.

315. "Plaza Restaurants on the Move," *Kansas City Star*, March 5, 1993, B:3; "Care for Some Rush with That Steak?" *Kansas City Star*, March 6, 1993, E:3.

Chapter 10

316. Ramos Vertical File: Biography A–E, "Charles Bryant," Missouri Valley Special Collections, Kansas City Public Library; Broomfield, *Food Biography*, 142–45.

317. Michael Wells, "How Did Kansas City Become 'Barbecue Capital of the World?,'" *Kansas City Star*, July 4, 2021, C:1.

318. Quoted in Bruce Brown, "A Legend's Heir, Embroiled Over Barbecue," *Washington Post*, July 12, 1990, www.washingtonpost.com.

319. *Black Smoke: African Americans and the United States of Barbecue* (Chapel Hill: University of North Carolina Press, 2021), 160.

320. "A Paradise for Wimpy," *Kansas City Times*, February 19, 1937.

321. "John Zachary Koury," *Kansas City Times*, January 12, 1966, 19; "James J. Nabhan," *Kansas City Star*, April 27, 1976; Gerald B. Jordan, "Sandwich Shop Packs 'em In," *Kansas City Star*, September 12, 1976, E:11.

322. Broomfield, *Food Biography*, 90–91.

323. *Black Smoke*, 110.

324. Author's interview with Marisha Brown-Smith, September 16, 2021. Much of this information comes from this interview with Brown-Smith.

325. "47 American Burger Spots You Need to Try Right Now," *Thrillist*, June 30, 2021, www.thrillist.com.

326. "This Iconic Trio of Diners Is Still the Talk of the Town," *Pitch*, June 3, 2010, www.thepitchkc.com.

327. Natalie Gallagher, "Town Topic," *Feast*, June 22, 2018, www.feastmagazine.com.

328. Author's interview with Ruby Morlan, October 13, 2021.

329. "James Brown Coe Obituary," *Kansas City Star*, December 5, 1998, B:5.

330. Morlan interview, October 13, 2021.

331. "Playboy's View of in Kansas City, Condensed from 'NO' by Calin Trillin in *Playboy Magazine*," *Kansas City Star*, August 6, 1972, 20.

332. Little advertising exists from Jess & Jim's earliest years, but when selling a pool table in 1941, the address given in a *Kansas City Star* advertisement was for Jess & Jim's Lunch, its original name; Jess and Jim's "Our History," www.jessandjims.com.

Index

INDEX

About the Author

Andrea Broomfield is a native Kansas Citian. She is a chairperson and professor of English at Johnson County Community College in Overland Park, Kansas, and the author of several articles and two books pertaining to food and history, *Food and Cooking in Victorian England: A History* and *Kansas City: A Food Biography.*

Visit us at
www.historypress.com